The Long Walk to Glastonbury
Via the Ridgeway, Avebury and Stonehenge

Stewart Harding

Acknowledgements

Thanks go especially to Martin Wride (Madhead) and Roger Bloomfield for being the best travelling companions a man could want and for providing their own 2022 commentaries and reminiscences of the walk some fifty years after the event. For anyone interested in astrological dynamics the fellowship of the walk was made up of one Aries (Squash) and two Leos (Madhead and Roger). Little wonder we so enjoyed our campfires and had no trouble lighting them.

Many thanks to Roger for taking on the task of producing route maps of the Walk with such good humour.

Thank you to all the cheerful and kind-hearted strangers who helped us on our way and especially the merry boys and girls of Avebury Trusloe who enlivened our stay in Avebury and whose company we enjoyed around our campfire.

Thanks also to all those many fine folk who read and enjoyed early versions of this tale serialised on the Facebook groups "Avalon/Glastonbury of the Heart" and "Ridgeway and Ancient Tracks of Britain" for their support and encouragement to publish the story in book form. Giles Watson, admin of the Ridgeway group, deserves special mention for his unstinting support.

Thanks to Dr Adam Stout, Glastonbury historian and writer, for his kindly blandishments to get my finger out and stop enjoying myself.

Thank you Greg Bint for the cosmic cover art.

Thank you Jeremy Moorhouse, writer, for sharing your self-publishing experiences with me.

Thank you Jenny Hardie for the colourising of photos.

The usual thanks to my wife Nicole who had to put up with my distractedness and occasional rants about the sheer bloody-minded difficulty of trying to do anything out of the ordinary.

Thank you Henry Harding for helping to steer me through the intricacies of self-publishing.

Is that everyone? I doubt it, so for anyone I have overlooked please accept my thanks and enjoy the general blessings of being part of life on Earth.

PART I

Reading to Avebury via the Ridgeway

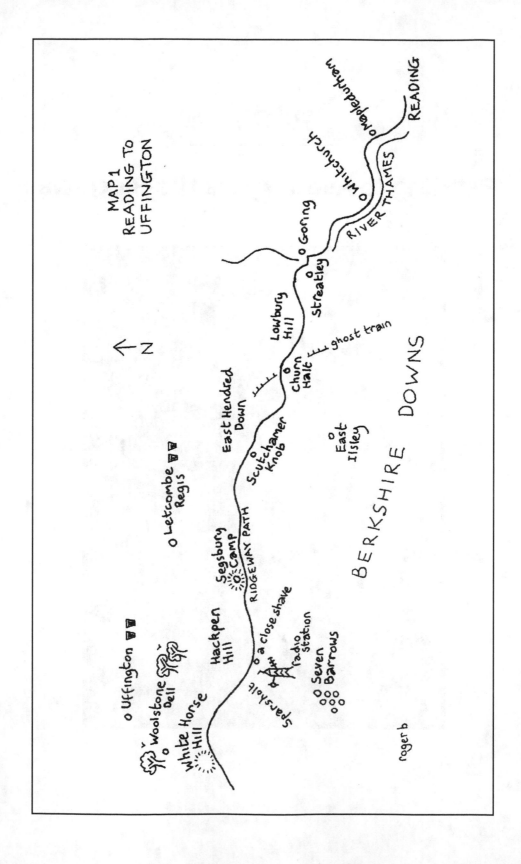

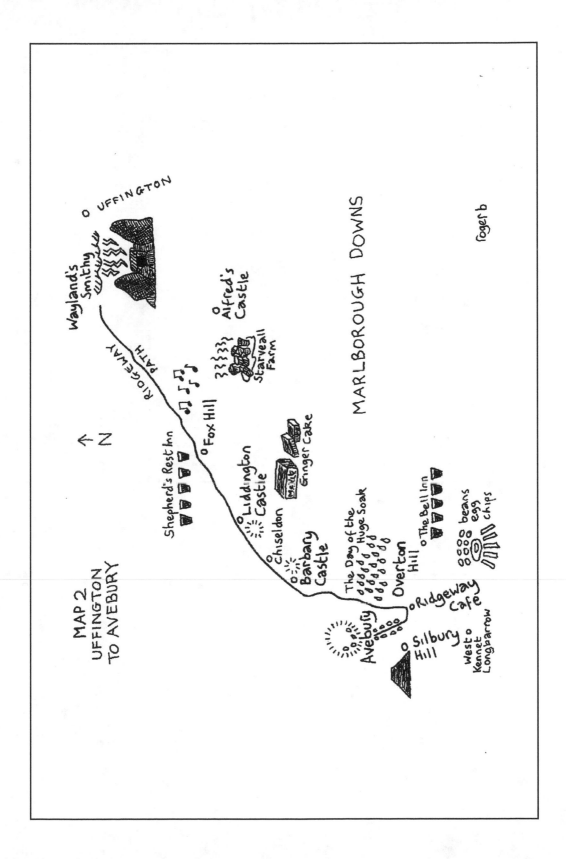

Open your front door and the road can take you anywhere

The story gets better as time goes on as the holy hippie weirdness grows. Honest. So, if you want to, please read on …

It was on this date, fifty years ago, that we three intrepid hippies, Squash, Madhead and Roger, set out on a mildly spiritual quest for the soul of Ancient Albion by walking from Reading to Glastonbury, to arrive in time for the summer Solstice. There follow entries from the daily diary I kept in a notebook made for me by Madhead. I have added a little ill-remembered commentary and fleshed out some of the entries for clarity.

To celebrate the 50th anniversary of the Walk, Madhead and Roger have added their 2022 observations to my 1973 diary entries from their own recollections. You have the choice of reading the diary straight through and going back to see what we thought of it all 50 years later or reading our reminiscences on each day's events as you go along. Up to you.

This would be our (nearly) 40 days and 40 nights living in the wild, thinly funded by about £20 between us, equivalent in value to maybe £250 in 2023.

We had made some basic preparations for this adventure. The weekend before we went out and bought the cheapest tent we could find. It was an orange two-man tent made of nylon and was therefore ostensibly waterproof and needed no flysheet, groundsheet built in and with a little mesh window at the back. None of us wanted to carry more than necessary. We each bought a Blacks' "Icelandic" feather and down sleeping bag that rolled up nice and small. We eschewed camping stoves and all that paraphernalia and equipped ourselves instead with billy-can for cooking, small lightweight wooden bowls which would serve as plate and cup, a metal spoon each for eating and a single wooden spoon for stirring the pot and, on our belts, dangled our sheath knives.

I had collected all the Ordnance Survey one inch to the mile maps that would cover our way to Glastonbury. Roger was well stocked up with brown rice, oats and miso paste and other exotic ingredients that gradually were revealed as time went on. As I didn't own a coat I had spent the previous week making one from a grey army surplus blanket, stitched up with thread I had painstakingly waxed by passing it through candle-melt. It was a crazy-looking thing that went over the head and had big floppy wizard's sleeves. We had all quit our jobs, looking forward to the joy of not having to go to work for a while.

All set and ready to go. I bade a fond farewell to my long-suffering mum. This time we both knew there was no coming back, unlike the previous times I had left home only to return licking my wounds.

Before leaving, Roger consulted the I Ching which gave us hexagram 60 Limitation - "the thrift that sets fixed limits upon expenditure". The moving lines gave us two possibilities - "sweet limitation brings good fortune" or "galling limitation". These in turn gave us a second hexagram 41 Decrease - "if a time of scanty resources brings out an inner truth, one must not be ashamed of simplicity" and, more ominously, "the text says that three persons journeying together are decreased by one" and we'll see if that did indeed come to pass ....

From the diary this day:

High cloud all over grey, wet but no rain. We met up at my mother's house in Emmer Green, on the northern outskirts of Reading, and went on our way in the early afternoon. I was completely taken with the hobbity notion that the road started at your front door and went forever on. Sun came out and stayed. Took a route down Gravel Hill and were in the countryside in five minutes, through Stokes's Farm at Bugs Bottom and up over Shepherd's Lane, crossing the main Woodcote Road and onto a footpath that took us through overgrown woods and around the top edge of perilous chalk-pits and long-abandoned quarries, down down to close to the Thames riverside. Walked an easy 11 miles along The Warren past spooky Mapledurham House and through the village taking a track there past Hardwick House to Whitchurch and on again, through Hartslock Woods, passing a gate to a house in the woods called Rivendell, the Last Homely House in The Lord of the Rings.

It was getting dark so we stopped in a woody glade by the river outside Goring where we made camp and lit a fire. From our campsite we could see the broad rising hump of the Berkshire Downs through the Goring Gap, whither we are bound. It felt like tomorrow we would be leaving the Shire and the adventure would really begin.

Gathered stinging nettle tops to add to the bubbling rice in the twilight, to the sound of a cuckoo and birds fussing before bedtime. Moon almost full. Roger meditating facing across the great river. Clear night, stars out. A duck croaks goodnight. Feeling happy being out here where I feel I belong.

More tomorrow ...

2022

Madhead: Do I want to be Madhead or Martin now? Happy to stay Madhead. My grandchildren think it's funny.

Nothing to add so far other than my boots, although newish, were monkey boots. While they looked cool, they were entirely inappropriate for the journey. It's a wonder they lasted.

Squash: Yes, we both bought monkey boots for the walk – cheap leather ankle boots with stout rubber soles, a poor man's Doc Martens but without the skinhead associations. Roger had proper Doc Martens. But the monkey boots turned out to be durable and comfortable.

Roger: I can remember talking about doing the walk, and the feeling of it being some kind of a pilgrimage, a quest for each and all. I decided I was going to shave my head once we were on our way and just before setting off I had my long hair cut short ready for that to happen.

I must have had a bit of money from some job or other and went into a camping shop in Reading to kit myself out for the life of a pilgrim dharma hobo, guided by the spirit of Jack Kerouac and tales of the Zen poet monks of China and Japan. A frame rucksack, a pair of Doc Marten boots, an "Icelandic" sleeping bag for kipping subzero and a black stormproof zip-up coat that rolled up to almost nothing.

I was 19 then and it's 50 years since our journey and I have nothing written of my own to refer to for my recollections. I did not keep a diary but I took along my little Olympus camera.

I remember the feeling of adventure, striding out from Reading, the Thames to our left. I have it in my head that we made our riverside camp in Hartslock Wood just upstream from Pangbourne and Whitchurch on that first night. Did we? I can picture it quite vividly.

Gimme dat old time religion, it's good enough for me, sang Captain Beefheart.

Leaving the Shire

Yesterday took our three hobbity heroes as far as the outskirts of Goring-on-Thames, home village of Danny La Rue. Today we venture onto the high places. I should say here that this was no testosterone-fuelled balls-out march or "hike" as practised by Yorkshiremen and other types of earnest fellows. This was more of a meandering exploration of place, time, meaning and pointlessness underpinned by an enthusiasm for ancient sites, the natural world and avoiding going to work. There is not always much of interest to report - most of the time it was walk, walk, walk, chop down wood, carry water - the sound of one hand clapping. As with all prolonged outdoor adventures, weather and food quickly become the major considerations, as you will see if you can be bothered to read on. Dot dot dot ...

From the diary:

Last night was one of the coldest I've spent anywhere, but sleeping curled into an S and spooning myself just about ensured my survival. I don't know which part of Iceland my Black's "Icelandic" sleeping bag was designed for - the geyser fields maybe. The lumpy pillow I made of my monkey boots and rolled-up jeans could do with some fine tuning too. Anyway the day dawned fine, cloudless and windless with a wet mist hanging over the river and dripping off the trees. After a breakfast of muesli and stewed tea we broke camp early and passed unseen through pretty Goring-on-Thames and over the bridge to Streatley and up the hill past Thurle Grange and onto the windy Ridgeway.

The first mile and a half is straight down on a whooshy ley line. Yellowhammers performing weird mating dances and skylarks and lapwings abound. Curiosity diverted us to Lowbury Hill camp, an ancient hillfort and, according to the O/S map, the later site of a Roman Temple of which no trace was there to see. There are dozens of tracks on this part of the Downs that all look like they might be the Ridgeway so it took us a while to find the route again.

Later surprised and delighted to stumble on the line of an abandoned railway, part of the old Great Western Railway Didcot to Newbury line, where the Ridgeway crosses a cutting on a bridge. We decided to camp down in the cutting near the site of the long vanished Churn Station, built as a private halt for a local nob and later serving a WWI rifle camp, to shelter from the wind and to imagine ghost trains steaming across this incredibly remote spot.

We made a superb dinner of wakame seaweed, leather top mushrooms, carrots, spuds and celery all stewed up with miso and delicately served with a jagged hunk of bread. After-dinner entertainment included Madhead prodding a leatherjacket and Roger playing with cheese-logs. Slowing down to this timescale is difficult and my thoughts repeatedly turn hopelessly carnal. Must be all the fresh air.

More tomorrow …

2022

Madhead: After the first day, which seemed just like an ordinary ten-mile nature hike, the second day became more of an adventure. The slowing down of time. The awakening of the senses. The easing into the environment. The food we cooked and ate began to become a focus to our endeavours.

Roger: Some of my offerings here might not be memories but imaginations of memories because I can't remember much! Yet. But there are feelings coming up as I relive the walk. Like the feeling of being on the ancient Ridgeway path. That long straight whoosh bit at the beginning, there's a photo, isn't there? Then that feeling. As we walk the path walks us. Yes the sound of the lapwings and the sky-larks. The sky and the earth and finding our rhythm of walking. Muscles starting to ache (well, mine were), rucksack straps starting to dig in.

Yeah, Churn Station, camped by the bridge. A sort of non-place in the wild, railway without rails. Not a place to shave my head, I remember thinking or saying. Our friend the billycan, oh boy, the simple feast after the trek.

Squash: I wonder how much, or how little, of the walk I would have remembered without the diary. Memory is a tricky thing, it likes to make epic sense by changing events, the order of things, the cast list, the places and recombining them into pictorial narratives in which we can emerge as heroes of our own destiny. Big up The Diary.

High skies and a low knob

Another pretty uneventful day on the Ridgeway, a place that feels on top of the world, where it's easy to imagine all the movements of menfolk, womenfolk, children and animals back and forth down the centuries and millennia, to battle, to farm, to make pilgrimage, to visit friends, to run away from something horrible approaching from east or west, to shelter in the great hillforts from raiders and invaders. The ancient trackway was like a smooth green motorway when I walked it three years before but is now narrowed by fences and often rutted and pitted by tractors as agriculture on the downs has been shifted by subsidies from sheep farming to arable and mechanisation has taken hold in a big way.

From the journal entry du jour:

Froze my bollocks off again all night but Madhead and Roger had good sound sleeps the bastards. Gonna wear my trousers tonight. After breakfast of muesli and hot milk we set out early across the Downs, sun beating down but the wind keeps cold from the south-east. Our path crossed by a disdainful country squire type on a huge stallion riding across the ploughed up Ridgeway. Can see how easily the nobs commanded and controlled the peasants, the combination of horse and man was tall, tall, tall – and intimidating, a tingle of traditional fear ran through me. Looking up at him looking down at us evoked uncomfortable tribal memory. You'd have to look up to these self-appointed overlords even while they gave you a bloody good thrashing.

Across Bury Down and up we went with the wind at our backs and horseflies in our faces, quiet we are, falling into the hypnotic rhythm of the walk. I burnt my arm on the fire this morning and it's stinging in the wind. Through East Hendred Down and past the Scutchamer Knob, an ancient round barrow that has been looted and half-destroyed so that only a low crescent remains in the undergrowth. Quite disappointing as knobs go. Barrow-wights howl and snicker in the trees and the breeze.

Reached Segsbury Camp, also called Letcombe Castle Hillfort, where we pitched up for the night. We left the gear and trotted down the hill to the Sparrow Inn in Letcombe Regis which was full of country folk Christ Arrr!. We ate bread, cheese and pickled onions and drank three pints. Straggled back up the hill in the dark. Only three pints and I'm pissed. Must be the country air.

Goodnight me, goodnight them.

2022

Madhead: Although the man on the horse was a posho, he was no friend to the farmer. Lesser mortals would take the long way and keep to the edge of the field in case they got shot at or something. Every time Mary and are out walking and come across a ploughed footpath, I always imagine I'm that man on the horse and tromp along the line of the path, scrunching everything underfoot. Same thing with field-edge paths. If the field is planted, I walk on the first two rows, breaking what I can. There are lots of cornfields down my way (to feed intensive cow prisons/units) and young maize makes a satisfying crunch as I go along. Particular farmers around here never spend time on the upkeep of footpaths and stiles. They are public enemies and need to be tamed. End of rant, back to the story. It was cold at night during the first week or so, but fatigue would help me sleep in spite of everything. I remember the Sparrow Inn in particular. Was it really three pints? Couldn't do that now – I'd be forever going to the bog in the night.

Roger:

racehorse stud farms on the downs
stretches and gallops
ripple flank. nostril snort
hooves thundering the chalk
we three, treading quietly

I'm going to have to look at the maps
all those names, I know them, I knew them

Squash: A pretty uneventful day but a perfect day for getting accustomed to walking wearing a backpack and for your body and mind to feel their way into travelling in the great windswept outdoors. The Ridgeway really does feel like walking over the top of the world. And then the pub to ease the tired legs.

A long walk and a close shave

Our three aimless adventurers are adjusting to the slower pace of life away from noise and traffic and concentrating on the thing in hand. They have yet to discover what the thing is, but they are definitely creeping up on something, probably.

From the diary:

A warm night at last so slept well apart from nightmarish vision of stabbing about 20 people with my pocket knife. Still, Roger's Buddhist teacher, Zengo, told him that you are all the characters in your dreams so I was basically stabbing 20 different versions of myself, thinning things out I guess. It's just inner conflict so that's alright then. There was a running full moon with clouds fleeting across – hmmm, thinking is this what was called a bombers' moon? Just imagine that. Dropping deadly explosions and rains of fire on people you don't know. The condensation in the tent is a bit extreme. It's a weird orange tent, weighs little but gives you a shower every morning. Nylon you see.

We went into Letcombe Regis for provisions. I'm worried about how much money we are spending but Madhead and Roger seem happy about it. We struggled back up Castle Hill to the Ridgeway in heavy sweat. I've always hated carrying a rucksack cos it weighs down the floaty lightness of youth but it does have everything I need in it. I should shut up. Madhead and Roger are carrying far more than me. We stopped on Rats Hill to remove our coats and I lost my beads. Roger later offered me his Tibetan prayer beads but I couldn't take them, they belong on him.

This part of the track climbs higher to 762 feet at the summit of Gramps Hill and down and up again a mile on above Childrey Warren, just past Folly Clump. There's a strong wind up here and fewer flies and birds, just the lonesome cry of the peewit and the distant song of the skylark. There's a profusion of bird's eye trefoil mingling with cowslips - very pretty - and occasional wind-bent thorns which are yet bare. There's a beautiful view up here atop Hackpen Hill of the Devil's Punchbowl and Crowhole

Bottom and, further over, a distant view of - yes – the huge cooling towers of Didcot Power Station which has been a constant landmark on this stretch. We started out hating its intrusion in the landscape but have become quite familiar with its alien presence. It's a landmark sure enough.

We decided to stop in the beechwood near the crossways for a fire and bowl of tea (we each have a bamboo bowl that serves for everything - food, drink, washing and hat). I mosied down to Sparsholt Radio Station which is very high security, probably with underground bunkers crammed with corned beef and sultanas IN THE EVENT OF NUCLEAR WAR. I just knocked on the door and the nice man filled the big collapsible water bottle for me. Water is a constant need and is a pain in the arse to carry but I should again shut up because Madhead carries it. Good man he is.

After our tea I shaved Roger's head at his insistence, part of his Zen letting go of vanity and material things. Was gonna whip off his eyebrows too but we decided that might have been taking things too far. It was a long job and used all the water so we decided to stay here for the night. I went back to the Radio Station for a refill but everyone had gone home. So I tried the door and bless me it opened, so I walked right in and filled the bottle up at the sink. I was tempted to explore a bit but it was all very MI5 Cold War in there with blinking lights, bleeps and whirring things and my arsehole started popping.

Gathered a load of deadwood while Roger was somewhere in the undergrowth meditating and getting used to his new head. Madhead and I sat around being Madhead and me, but slightly different versions of ourselves. We decided we need to spend less money each day or we are going to be potless before long. Poot.

We made a nice dinner of roasted sesame seeds, brown rice, carrots and onions, and nettle tops. Then I had a whittling accident with my Swiss Army knife, sliced my thumb down to the bone, lots of my precious blood spilling out. We washed it, dressed it and then ignored it. Later, sitting in our first rainshower we exchanged ghastly ghouly tales and put ourselves to bed.

2022

Madhead: Brave Roger and his new head of ghost-hair. Lawks! All of a sudden Roger became more mysterious somehow and the whole 'quest' took on a deeper meaning. This was some serious shit. I was never brave enough to do that, even though I trusted Squash to not cut me too much. Looking back, shaving my head would have saved a lot of faff, what with having to wear headbands or ponytails in my long, though meagre, hair all the time.

Then there was that water bottle! I'd made a bag and shoulder strap for it from an old hessian sack which seemed like a good idea until the bottle was full of water and thus became a millstone. (Five litres? Probably still a gallon in 1973.) The bag was meant to keep the water cool. It didn't. Another wonderful thing was being able to light cooking fires willy-nilly across the land and then stamp them out and replace the turf so as to leave little or no trace. Proper backwoodsman stuff.

The tent was very orange so at some point we named it Saffron Cottage. If I close my eyes, I can still see, feel, hear, and smell it. It was very much our mobile home.

Roger: I am sitting here forty-eight years later contemplating the shaving of my head, a memory which hasn't been absorbed through the filter beds of forgetfulness back into the universe. Kneeling there, surrounded by trees as my witness, as Squash wielded the safety razor without nicking me once. Giving up my long locks and shedding my inner shackles - maybe.

We probably talked lots about doing the walk and had our various ideas and dreams about why we were doing the walk, but I think once we'd taken the first step, we were doing the walk because we were doing the walk. It was the mystic thing. Anything profound, deep, significant, hilarious, whatever, tends to come up of its own accord, and it did. No need to explain. Anyway, most people understand the ancient and innate urge to go for a walk.

Shaving one's head might need more of an explanation but really I just wondered what it would be like to do what Buddhists do. I liked it so much I never did it again! I'd also learned the aimless practice of Zazen, Zen sitting, and liked it so much I did it for the rest of my life. My head was as soft and as smooth as a dharma bum. Until the stubble grew. And I kept my beard just in case.

The Sparsholt Radio Station sounds cool, I don't remember that.

Squash: Shaving Roger's head was much more laborious than I expected. Who would think a head is so much bigger than a chin? But it was fun, seeing his gleaming white bonce emerging into the daylight, something it hadn't felt in 19 years. The whole ritual was conducted with holy grace and not a little sniggering.

This was the day I learnt that you should whittle in the direction away from you unless you are a master craftsman. I wasn't. I also learnt that thing about gaining access to places you shouldn't, that mostly all you have to do is pretend that you belong and you can saunter right in.

The Fools on the Hill

Shaving Roger's head yesterday was a marker for the increasing spirituality permeating the souls of our three lovable fools. And a good laugh of course. As the minds quietened, the senses perked up and the sacred nature of this mission started to insinuate itself. All that was needed was a sign or two, a revelation or a stray meatball striking the side of the head for something profound to awaken. Read on ...

From the diary this day:

Woke up with a bladder like a brick, an overwhelming sensation of being back in Holland and a refreshing shower of condensation, much of it generated by Madhead who had been panting his way up to the climax of a wet dream but didn't quite make it. Hahaha. A thick mist early cleared quickly to warm still sunshine. After muesli we toasted some bread on sticks on the fire. Broke camp late after much messing about, skirting the woods south and onto the road towards Lambourn. South along Eastmanton Down and taking the track through Pit Down to Seven Barrows, though we counted eight. There was just one tree, an amazing old but quite small beech tree on the largest tump with branches growing out and in again, like lattice-work. This one only beginning in leaf while all the other beeches around here are in full sail.

We looned around a while in the sunshine and I caught up with my diary atop a tump while Madhead tried to outstare the beech tree.

Later taking the steep hot track around Crag Hill and up Woolstone Down to the highpoint of Idlebush Barrow. Beautiful views all around and a feeling of triumph for there, a mile north-west, the steeply scarped slope of Uffington Castle. Four days from Streatley to Uffington – gotta be a record for the least vigorous expedition ever undertaken on the Ridgeway. Overtaken by snails, the Ice Age moved quicker. Hey ho.

A slice each of bread and miso and then on towards that familiar and inspiring camp. Losing the track a little we stumbled over a few fences in a cooling shower. Crossing the huge grassy enclosure, over the outer ramparts and there! suddenly a view to dazzle, right across the Vale of White Horse. We paid a visit and homage to the White Horse or Dragon, whatever it is, and took the steep path to Dragon Hill, where St George was supposed to have slain the dragon. Some Christian bullshit intended to supersede age-old pagan beliefs, him coming all the way from Turkey just to mess with our pagan dragon.

Took the hill road down towards Woolstone where we are camped in the little beech and elm wood in Woolstone Dell which nestles pubicly in the crotch of the hills, absorbing all the stray magic energy that flows through this special place along with a stream of the clearest water. This little wood explodes with life. Roger thinks it's enchanted, magnifying the cosmic energy that collects in the Manger. Settling down to silence after erecting the tent (now named Saffron Cottage) and collecting firewood, the birds resumed their business of singing their heads off. I redressed the wound in my thumb which seems to be healing ok. Dinner's bubbling away in the billy-can, miso stew with vegetables and seaweed. Food is a massive treat when you don't have much. Such happiness I felt feeding the fire and watching the billy boil.

After dark we chewed Roger's ginseng and laboured back up the hard climb to White Horse Hill. It was a beautiful crystal clear night. Lying spread-eagled on the summit of Dragon Hill watching stars move and feeling that the lying down could be any direction upside down spinning turning or dropping. It seemed to me a silver rope of popping lights occasionally flicked down from the stars. The dark hills commanding quiet and humility. Lying in the chalk ear of the dragon. Closing my eyes first I saw in my mind's eye a white horse or was it a unicorn? Then the ear became the ear that hears the eternal silence that exists behind all noise, and I listened and became part of that silence. If silence can be heard it rings like a high endlessly distant sustained ding from a tuning fork. How so ever noisy the world is, there exists a deep black silence behind and beyond. Sitting on the chalk eye of the dragon the eye became the eye that perceives the nothing behind all things and I looked and became part of that nothing. The wind became the wind of change, blowing this way and that, always the same, always different, going on forever. All these things were inside my head and outside my head.

Found our way back to the camp by starlight, using that trick my brother showed me of staring straight ahead in the dark so that your peripheral black and white vision lights your path. Weird but works.

2022

Madhead: Blimey. Four days! By the time we got to White Horse Hill, Dragon Hill and Woolstone Dell, it felt like it had been weeks – if not a lifetime (relatively speaking). I was expecting more from the ginseng, to be honest, having tried various things previously (ahem). However, just the buzz of being there was enough. Lying outside in the dark is good for the soul. It's dark at night where I now live in the middle of Somerset because there are no street lights for miles. It's fabulous to be out there in starshine and moonlight, even for an old codger. Often, when I'm walking home at night, I turn my torch off, blink a few times, and go forward with that same peripheral vision trick. It does help to be on a road though, the verges soon tell you if you're veering too much!

Roger:

'There's a natural mystic flowing through the air
If you listen carefully now you will hear'

What does a beech tree do if it can't spread its saucer of roots outwards because it's on a small round barrow? The unfamiliar act of growing roots downwards instead brings on a crazy dance of branches above? For a couple of hundred years or so. An ordinary hillock and the beech tree might have given up but here on an ancient barrow things might be different. These ancient places, historians scratching their chins. Seven barrows, three fools, two hairy, one bald.

Arriving at the Vale of the White Horse we don't need to believe in anything, just stopping in our tracks and gazing, that first sight of the sweeping curve of hillside leading out to the horizon, brings a huge reverence, a prayer as big as the sky, and maybe an urge to scrape the turf and draw a dragon. The nestling trees of Woolstone Dell welcome us: 'we like you, you can stay'...

Gathering wood and making fire, cooking our food in the bubbling billy.

Then we climb back up in the starlight to be with the Horse of the Sparkling Sky.

Four days journey on foot to get here, then make our stay.

Learning how to make friends with a place, tread lightly, listen carefully

Squash: I remember vividly that night, lying on the White Horse on top of the hill. The revelation I didn't put in the diary, but that stays with me still, was the realisation that because it was night-time I was lying on the BOTTOM of the planet and if gravity let go I would plunge forever into the infinite black void below. We are so accustomed to perceiving the sky as always above us in the direction UP. On the White Horse I experienced the powerful sensation of peering DOWN into a bottomless black pit sprinkled with stars. Spooky.

Popping an angry balloon

Yesterday was a day of unexpected thrills for our wandering simpletons – inconclusive wet dreams, looning on a tump in proper sunshine and plungement into the void in the crystal dark of a White Horse night - and today, being Saturday, is altogether different. A day for homely chores and soaking up the magical mystical vibe of Woolstone Dell which we like very much.

From de diary this day:

Woke late to the soothing coo-cooing of dozens of wood pigeons. Left Roger and Madhead in bed awhile, while I re-lit the fire and got the last of the muesli together. Shopping day today, so we wandered into the village of Woolstone and popped into the White Horse Inn. O boy o boy the landlord in there was one seriously provocative sarcastic fucker, before we'd said a word he was shooting off his humour about our "spiritual bullshit" and "hippy swansong" in an unwanted and unwarranted spiteful rant. But, but me some buts Mister Shagnasty, there is in you some sour grapes, some unfulfilled dream, some unrequited love eating away at you I reckon. But when we stood up to him and he realised we weren't to be easily cowed he cooled it a bit, then cooled it a lot. He was okay in the end, still sarcastic but less aggressive, a spikily witty man overfull of himself. I quite liked him. He called Madhead "Buggerlugs" which was good. This little scene seems to have brought Roger down, but I don't know exactly in what way, although I do have an inkling.

We went on up the road into Uffington past some of the oldest cottages I've seen anywhere, looking like they grew out of the ground and were slowly settling back into it, grass and moss in the ragged grey thatch. Uffington village is a weird mixture of very old and tasteless new. Did our shopping in the village stores, served by a helpful gent who gave us a nice big bag of past-it, slightly wizened swedes. Went into another pub in Uffington whilst waiting for the other grocery shop to open, as it was presently closed for lunch. Drank a couple of pints which made us feel all weak, silly and helpless and made our senses wide open to the brass-band music that was blaring from the radio. Brass bands never sounded so surreal. It was as if every note was a new one and the arrangements of the tunes were psychedelically complicated and labyrinthine.

After this little detour into semi-civilisation it was wonderful to get back to Woolstone Dell and scrambled eggs. It started to rain softly so we crawled into the tent for a gentle snooze to the pitter-patter of the rain and the gurgle of the stream below. Madhead and Roger are now pottering around outside getting the grits together and I'm just going out to help, soon as I finish this day's diary. For dinner we had mashed swede and potatoes, sesame seeds, miso, seaweed and bread. Roger meditated for a while in my bicycle cape, the perfect shape to cover a lotus position in the rain. He was a bright yellow pyramid, surmounted by a dome of bald wet head. We sat around the fire really late.

I started a letter to Anne before bed.

2022

Madhead: Of all the bars in all the world ...

Vivid memories of the pub and of the blokes who asked us if we'd washed in the stream because it allegedly was the water supply to the village. Of course we didn't. There is a photo of us not washing in the stream.

What stands out is the fact that we spent more money with the landlord who insulted us than with the man who gave us the swedes. Always had a soft spot for brass bands. They are the epitome of working-class music-making. My Grampy played the euphonium in the Charles Hill Shipyard Silver Band. Despite its size, the euphonium has a very sweet baritone sound not unlike my singing actually.

Roger: I have no recollection whatsoever of this day, but I remember Woolstone Dell, amazing magical woodland. I hope it is still there, unharmed and beautiful.

Squash had a way of dealing with confrontational provocative sarcastic fuckers, by being more of a provocative sarcastic fucker than they were, but much better at it, and delivered with a sort of non-combative eloquence... this could have a sort of disarming and even levelling effect.

I was in awe of this skill. Worthy of any bardic contest I would say.

Also, I was just imagining coming across somebody sitting in a wood, in the rain, with a bald wet head, face neutral, sticking out of a bright yellow pyramid.

Squash: I have heard Madhead singing and it is not unlike the sweet tone of the euphonium. I now have no recollection of who Anne is/was. I was obviously at least slightly romantically involved with her but of her memory I have none. I find this forgetfulness odd and disturbing. Maybe she still has the letter, maybe she pines for me yet. Maybe I made her up as a sort of virtual camping girlfriend.

If you had to typify our characters I think you would have to conclude that Squash was the bold one, Madhead was the gleeful one and Roger was the mysterious one. Of course though, being happy together, we three also picked up the quintessence of these traits from each other, as fond friends do. This combination of attributes enabled us to collectively deal with whatever trials and weirdnesses came our way. Pretty much anyway.

And on the seventh day they rested, lazy bastards

From the diary on this Sunday:

Madhead dreamt strange dreams last night including a bit where a hippo crawled into another hippo's mouth to suck off the slime. I dreamt about junkies in the Liberal Party and a man yelling "you're just trying to be a Guru B" about a thousand times. Roger dreamt he had to hammer newspaper until the print came off.

Breakfast was porridge followed by boiled egg on toast. Delicious!

Sat around lazy day - rained again - whittling and wandering looking for birds' nests and stuff. Then we went across the little log bridge to the outfall of the spring and had the most amazing invigorating freezing cold water wash and hair wash.

Later as we were drying our hair by the fire a growing raucous row of shouting and branches breaking approached from the entrance to the Dell. Bears? Visitors? Fuck me, a big bunch of tomfooling greasers. Adrenalin pumping, on with the sheath knives just in case – in case of what? Anything I guess.

"Howdy" says me as they crunch and crash into our little camp. "Welcome to our camp" says Roger, spreading his arms expansively. Thirteen greasers! In this enchanted Dell, all of a sudden, thirteen grinning greasers. From up on the hill they'd seen the trickle-plume of smoke rising from the woods and came to investigate. They were bikers from Swindon. Fortunately my old rocker persona jumped out from inside me, I knew their kind, was one of them before my hippy epiphany and all the dope and acid, knew they were just good old boys who liked to have wild times and fun. So we talked a little about bikes and runs to Swanage and Santa Pod raceway and other such nonsense and about rockers I knew from when I worked in the bikers' cafes - the Viking in Reading and the Buccaneer in Didcot - five years ago. Some of the young rockers I'd known had since become big wheels in the Wessex chapter of the Hells Angels and this crowd knew of them by reputation. Phew, stroke of luck, our new friends became respectful and amenable.

Pull up a leaf to sit on lads.

Roger played mine host of our woody grove and brewed some tea and passed it round in our bowls and shared out the biscuits we'd scored yesterday, each taking a slurp and handing the bowls around. Hahaha, if you go down to the woods today you're sure of a big surprise … today's the day the Teddy Boys have their picnic. After some initial awkwardness they, and we, settled down and they began joking and entertaining us in greaser fashion, all bumptious bouncy good humour. After they'd scoffed all our biscuits they split with good wishes on all sides - thanks for the tea and biccies, enjoy your walk, don't give up. Far out. Friendliness, sharing and respecting "the other" smoothed the way.

Dinner was the rest of the wrinkled swedes boiled up with carrots and onions with Marmite and miso, some steamed nettle tops and a hunk of cheese and bread. Dinner over, we break camp and bid beloved Woolstone Dell sad and fond farewells. The wood gave us welcome and gently spoke of time to leave. We left it uninjured and expect to be welcomed back some distant day. Collect water from the spring and scramble scramble clunk we're on the road again. Through the field, past the youthful cattle, over the magic hump of Dragon Hill for the last time. Calf-stretching up the steep road with that 10 lbs of water too. Car-park late Sunday afternoon crowded at the top and an ice-cream van. Roger treated us to a cornet each. Nice.

Back on the Ridgeway it was an easy mile or so to electro-magnetic cosmic charging whoosh whoosh zeep accumulator Waylands Smithy. Decided to pitch the tent on the long axis of the barrow.

Went silly - went out went in fell out fall in collect wood giggle he suggested pitching the tent at the accumulator end of the barrow on its axis bold as love. Huffed up a little fire for tea and ate crunchy peanut butter sandwiches. The lights of Swindon twinkle silently away in the west. We're on a ley-line. Goo goo glub. Lay down to sleep but weird flashes and crackles kept me alert. Rolled a fag and, through our little mesh window, watched an incredible lightning storm over westways, over Swindon, splitting the sky most of the night.

2022

Madhead: The greasers! After my initial adrenalin rush and anal fluctuations, it all turned into a quaint tea party. The only odd thing was that they all seemed to be wearing their school shoes. All black and mostly polished. I didn't mention it at the time though.

Wayland's Smithy was a whole different kettle of fish. There is a continual astral hum to the place so I guess that's why they buried their worthies there. The lightning over Swindon was only for our benefit. Wow. What a night.

Roger:

'One pleasant summer's morning, when all the flowers were springing-o, nature was adorning, and all the small birds singing-o'

But what of nature in tooth and claw and adrenalin? ...

Our peaceful, eternal, fireside reverie is broken by the sounds of rough shouting crashing through the bushes towards us:

'Rockers! PUT ON YOUR KNIVES!' Squash says with a voice of quiet but firm authority, reaching for his belt and its sheath knife, Madhead does the same as if he's completed rigorous training for just this sort of situation. Then there's me: what the FUCK, I don't have a sheath knife! But I have a BALD HEAD! So our biker boys are met with two grinning wild haired warriors quietly ready for anything and an unarmed welcoming Buddhist comedian. I offer them tea.

Isn't the nervous system amazing! 0 – 60 in 3 seconds!

So, Madhead noticed they were all wearing their school shoes? I don't remember that. It was Sunday, so perhaps they were choirboys out in the wild after Morning Service. Nothing is as it seems.

Wayland's Smithy. Huge stones at its entrance. Serious earthwork. Grave. Or was it?

I went there one afternoon years after our Walk but still years ago (such is the time span I can now encompass) and there was a full-on ceremony in progress, Celtic, Druidic, something. There were small fires lit at various points around the mound and people in white robes, and flower bedecked garlands and ceremonial staffs, incantations being said or sung. A very old man with a long white beard presiding. It was all very beautiful and not solemn. I felt a little intrusive but stayed a while looking on and no-one told me to go away.

That night we stayed there, where to pitch the tent, indeed, placement felt significant. Then the electrical storm. I found that if I parted my jaws very slightly, my fillings clicked, sparks jumping the gap.

Squash: When you are out in the wild anything can happen and you have to be prepared. In this scenario we see two opposite but complementary approaches to potential hostility. Firstly you show that you are unlikely to be a push-over and could be a dangerous opponent and secondly, with lightning speed, you proffer a welcome and show a willingness to be friendly – so long as your space and person is respected. Respect goes a long way in the meetings of strangers. Tea and biscuits generally help too. Roger's expansiveness took them by surprise and was, in its own way, a manifestation of power of a different, greater, kind. Thus we see and learn from each other.

Wayland's Smithy was altogether another manifestation of power, one beyond the scope of our understanding. Awesome place.

A change of mood on this, the start of our second week on the Ridgeway

From the diary:

Woke up feeling drained - had a good sleep, eventually, while the electrical storm fizzed and crackled on, but felt weak anyway. Porridge this morning in the sunshine.

Broke camp and set off through a host of clamouring schoolchildren drawing their pictures of Wayland's Smithy. They barely registered our departure, must think it's natural for three wanderers to appear from nowhere and wander off. West along the Ridgeway and turned off south towards Alfred's Camp near where King Alfred defeated the Danes in the Battle of Ashdown. Halfway there the path had been planted so we had to trample the crops. There's a heavy chemical smell rising. At Alfred's Camp, just a low-banked enclosure, we shared an orange and had a look at a big pile of discarded weedkiller cans. Yuk. We could see down below us Ashdown Park House, an old hunting estate which looked impossibly smart and other-worldly out here in the rough. Then out on the road back towards the Ridgeway. Spirits sinking all the way, there's something wrong in the air. This farmer seems to have invested his efforts in everything anti-life. Oversprayed crops, ploughed up paths, old farm machinery rusting away by the side of the track and a dead crow hanging by the neck on a fence. This is a horrible sight and I doubt very much it deters crows, them being wily knowing birds. Sickening and unnecessary. Any self-respecting crow wouldn't want to feed on such tainted land anyway. The name of the farm? Starveall Farm. It figures.

Continued a weary downcast walk to Fox Hill, overlooking King Edward's Place, a spread-out riding stables looking smart. The stink of chemicals is accompanied by the stink of money around here and it is unpleasant. Camped in a scraggy and unhappy strip of beechwood, much despoiled by man, but we found a sheltered nook which wasn't so bad. Morale low and disconsolate vibe. Had dinner early to try to cheer us. Usual thing, roasted sesame seeds, brown rice, potatoes, onions, cheese and miso.

Whittled for a while and went to the nearby Shepherd's Rest Inn by the crossroads, where a minor road to Aldbourne crosses the Ridgeway. The public bar was a bizarre mixture of "almost" things – almost a waiting room, a florist's shop, a pub, a gaming room but not quite any of them. Jose, the landlady, somehow archetypical of country lonely pub widow or spinster, friendly but faded and exhausted. Living and digging in the past when she was probably a glamorous chorus girl, singer or frustrated actress. There were some far out people though, old and earthy, mixed with odd outsiders who had washed up in this backwater, old beautiful losers. We had a ploughman's lunch out of greed and chocolate.

Our food rations are very small and clearly not enough to feed us properly. Finding more and more that our very Yang salty miso-fuelled diet is provoking a craving for sweet things. Roger got fed up in the pub and split but came back later which was nice. Roger meditates every day and is searching his spiritual path and seems to find interaction with tired earthbound souls trying. We rapped with the landlady - the inn used to be called the Totterdown Inn, some of it, the lounge, is 500 years old. The shepherds had a pound across the lane and used to go in the pub for an occasional piss-up at various times of the year, an uproarious gathering of lonely sheep-herders. Got talking to another old guy, a retired journalist, about the old Ridgeway and the posh theatre and Wembley Stadium owner cum stockbroker who lived in King Edward's Place. He told us he committed suicide over money troubles and became a millionaire the next day. Hey ho. Sounds unlikely pub-talk but who knows? On the wall was a cutting from an old Sunday Express which was a print of his last article. Amazing, detached, sad, forgotten, dying, end of life gazeback. We talked some more about holy tramps who were, apparently, common in these parts. Seems we are following the footsteps of tradition.

Split at closing time, five pints full and mad with it. Built a roaring good fire at the camp and bashed out some howling music to relieve our troubled souls.

2022

Madhead: The morning after was very weird. It was as if all our energy had been drained. Perhaps it would have been better to have slept at the other end of Wayland's mound.

Walking through Starveall Farm was the absolute low point of the whole journey for me. All the little pellets of Nitram fertiliser (ammonium nitrate) speckled over the fields like tiny hailstones. Mind you, the smell of the brown stuff the local farmers use round here can get a bit much at times.

Didn't we go mad in the pub! I don't remember how much we drank. Five pints d'you say? No wonder we had no money for food. The most I can remember is that the Champion Jack Dupree song, *Drinkin' Wine Spodie-Odie*, was a feature of our boogie-woogie sing-song that night. It almost became our anthem. Every time I hear it now, I'm taken straight back to that very campfire.

Roger: It's amazing to read Squash's journal. I recall some things quite clearly, others I've probably imagined to fill the gaps, but many are just feelings, no pictures.

Along with my companions I too felt like my batteries had been emptied the next morning, strange feeling of having made it through the night, and awaking empty handed, the tithe for daring to camp at the Smithy maybe. At some point on the walk I started to thank each place we stayed. Just a gesture, a bow, a word. Holy tramp the earth.

And then the track led to the poisoned earth of Starveall Farm, where there was no grace, just bad medicine, ill-at-ease.

I can imagine I didn't find tarrying at the Totterdown Inn an attractive proposition for lifting my spirit, though neither was sitting on my own in an unhappy strip of beechwood, so I returned sheepishly and partook of the ale, the ointment of merriment, bellowing the loudest probably in our midnight choir.

Didn't we discover on more than one occasion, like, two occasions, that singing *Sunshine of Your Love* and the rain cleared up? But see, like all good magic, use it too much and it stops working.

Squash: Yes, the beer intake does seem a trifle extravagant but at least it was cheaper then than now. A pint of beer was marginally more expensive than a loaf of bread in 1973 and now it's four times the price. Tax the proles. Even so, five loaves would probably have been better for us than five pints each – fifteen loaves and no fishes! Our tired souls must have needed the nourishment of drink, laughter and company that day and damn the expense.

Barbarians at the gate

Yesterday was a sad day for our tripping trio - until they got pissed and yowled at the night that is. Let's see what today on the Ridgeway brings. Read on, dot dot dot

From the old diary this day:

Good sleep, breakfast of salty porridge with raisins and Mu tea.

Packed up, along the road past last night's pub where shepherds, liars and layabouts rested and over the M4 Motorway bridge, staring in wonder at all the vehicles racing past beneath and thinking shit this is going on all the time, all these people hithering and thithering. To what purpose? We shrugged and went way on up to the largeness of Liddington Camp hillfort. Fine views over Liddington and far back to Uffington Castle and Wayland's Smithy whence we had come. Shared an orange and then Madhead produced his sweet surprise - tada! - three Swizzels lollies, flying saucers on sticks! How does he do it? Him Magic Man. Leaving the hillfort the road goes down down down the hill to the curmudgeonly-looking housing estate outskirts of Chiseldon across a busy major road. After days in the wild wind of the Ridgeway the traffic hurtling past seems senselessly manic, noisy and pointless. Found a little shop and bought groceries and an amazing ginger cake which we gobbled immediately on the pavement like starving dogs. Nice.

Back on the road, on the track, down the track, then up up up 879 feet (it says on the map) to the remote and somehow barbaric Barbury Castle which is also called Barbary Castle. These hillforts variously described as Castle or Camp, as if no-one can make up their minds what they are, Not just a camp matey, not with all these massive defensive ditches and ramparts around a huge windswept grassy enclosure, must've been a place of refuge for people and animals when raiders were about. It's hard to imagine the sheer amount of work that went into building these places but, for sure, there was a pressing good reason for doing it.

Pitched the tent here on a slope, it's all slopes here, in the blowy open, and scratched enough firewood from the windblown clump of beeches in the nearby cow-field. I love beech trees for the way they look and the way their wood willingly and brightly burns. Roger went up the track for water but came back empty - no-one in anywhere.

Checking the map, I went off to Barbury Castle Farm in the hollow below, near a mile distant. Enjoyed trucking along with no rucksack, on my own in my home-made floppy blanket coat and singing that lovely song, *The Castle Far*, that goes:

The night is cold, the castle far, a forest lies between
my mind runs on and conjures scenes of love that might have been

My steed is lame, my lance is broken, my helmet cleaved in twain
the perils of the battle's past, the evil serpent slain

Perhaps the dawn will see me home
and from the gates they'll run
Keen hands will lift me from my horse
and fife will sound with drum

The night is cold, the castle far, my prize not love but fame
And she for whom the fight was won will never bear my name *

* "The Castle Far" from the 1970 album *Matthews' Southern Comfort* by Matthews' Southern Comfort

Day and few-day old calves stopped to scrutinise me. Beautiful babies. The farm notice spelled Barbary Farm. Weird. Barbarians at the gate. Inside, the farmstead is this ramshackle old flint and brick farmhouse, all ragged and some windows out, and a pond and a nanny-goat and loads of scruffy kids (human) running about. Farm people good easy young hip country ones, all friendly filled up the water bottle and insisted on bringing me back up to the Castle in an old Transit van. Wish he'd gotten out the tractor though, like he was gonna - would've been good to see the look on the faces of Roger and Madhead as I returned in my lofty magnificence. "Thanks a million man, cheerio". "It's nothing, and watch out for that freckly faced bull, he'll have you, soon as look at ya". "Yeah, right, thanks. Sure will." Don't fancy being shagged to death by a rampant bull even if he has got cute freckles.

Dinner was boiled onions and carrots, peas (luxury!), Marmite, bread and cheese. You'd think we'd get sick of these boiled dinners but we didn't. They were always delicious and hearty, a hungry edge being on our appetites. We had noticed too the effect of this wholegrain and vegetable diet on our bodies. Each morning I'm delivered of a perfectly formed, smooth, moist, firm turd which snipped cleanly and wiped its own arse. Bog paper, pah, don't need it no more.

After dinner a brilliant high flying clear sky, sunset clouds intricate fluffy castles in the air but now gathering gloom, wind getting up a little, specks and flecks of rain. Inside the tent we scurry and then ... rain, rain, rain ...heavier ... heavier ... heavier ... ridiculously heavy, unbelievably heavy, absurdly heavy, the heaviest rain I've been in a tent out of in. Heavy heavy man.

2022

Madhead: It's funny but I don't remember the rain at all. A bit like schoolboy summer days – always warm and sunny and long. Maybe I do remember the rain but it's hidden away like private tears.

Barbury Castle was a high point (ahem) though. As well as being very close to the sky, it gives that feeling of magnificence in man's endeavours. All grand hilltop earthworks have it. Along with Avebury, Silbury Hill and Stonehenge of course. All that effort to produce a mystery. There are two sets of earthworks on White Sheet

Down near Mere in Wiltshire. One Stone Age and one Iron Age. The Iron Age fort is nearer to us in time than it is to the Stone Age one but they are both massive, and still mysterious.

Roger:

Barbury Castle
Barbary Castle
Barbara Castle!

Food:
Salty porridge and raisins, yeah!
Mu tea, yeah!
Three Swizzels lollies, yeah!
Flying saucers on sticks, yeah!
Ginger cake, yeah!
Boiled onions and carrots, yeah!
Marmite, bread and cheese, yeah!

And two sort-of haikus I saw in your text:

all slopes here, in the blowy open
firewood from the windblown clump

up the track for water
but came back empty
no one in, anywhere

I remember sitting next to the tent on the slope and talking to Madhead about something, and Squash returning from Barbary Farm bearing water and a story of the folk there.

Squash: And that's the memory-jogging power of the Diary. Jog jog it goes. Rain rain it goes.

The Day of the Huge Soak from Barbary Castle to Overton Hill

The diary sniffs and says:

Morning came and everything was wet from last night's downpour. It's very cosy in a two-man tent with three of us, the rain hammering down and us scrunched together in the middle to avoid a soaking. Still, it wasn't raining now, just a few flecks of wet in the squally wind. Managed with patience to light a damp sizzling fire while Madhead and Roger went to Upper Herdswick for water. Our fire-lighting skills have so far been a match for the weather. Breakfast of oats, nuts and raisins with hot milk.

The sky was grey and low and rain started up again as we set out for the last leg of The Ridgeway to Overton, where it takes a great exposed curve from west to south around the shoulder of the Downs. Not too bad at first, a trifle moist, but gradually the wind increased and so did the rain, before long pounding and stinging into our faces. Like everyone everywhere we didn't put on our waterproof jackets until we were already wet and these just funnelled the water down onto our jeans above the knee and, by capillary action, ratcheted it up gradually to our goolies which did the sensible thing and retracted into the warmth of our bodies. My trusty old bicycle cape running torrents onto my stinging, chafing thighs.

Suitably neutered we pressed on, a real narrow-eyed, teeth-gritted splodgy plod for mile on wretched mile until the round barrows and the Ridgeway Cafe at the crest of Overton Hill on the A4 London to Bath Road greyly emerged through the watery landscape. Soaked and saturated we were. Shelter! Sanctuary! What a welcome sight! We stayed in there for three hours. Egg chips and beans, fried bread, bread and butter, rhubarb pie and custard, a bun and five cups of tea. Wrote six postcards between us and a letter to Chris while listening to the Who's *Mama's got a squeeze box* on the jukebox – someone in there liked it so much they kept putting it on.

Not all that keen to venture back outside but we had dried out a little and so walked here and there zigzag in a faint drizzle to West Overton, thinking to leave checking in to the great stone circle at Avebury until the morrow. Pitched miserable sodden tent in the squelchy leafmould in the knotted overgrown woods on White Hill. Don't know if woods in the rain are wetter or drier than being in the open. Somehow stumbling, snagging and tripping through the brambly undergrowth, we were wetter than ever. Clothes, sleeping bags, monkey boots, ground sheet all soaked. Sat glum in the tent amid the drips and splashes, avoiding looking into each other's faces for fear of the despair that might be lurking there.

Bollocks to this, come on. We shot off to the pub in West Overton, the Bell Inn, a quiet pub seemingly a bit down on its luck. Met two guys, Bernie and John. Had a ploughman's and 5 pints. Bernie knew people from the Queen's Head in Reading, our old freaks' hangout - Jane and others - also Mike Dancey from Bath and Lynn and Joe and Ian and Mad Maggie from Glastonbury. The hippy world within a world. John knew of Pete Hickey's big Freewheelers motorcycle gang reputation, and I knew him as a nice younger bloke in the Viking Café from my rocker days. Men do change.

There was a bus stop and shelter opposite the pub and we ruminated that we could catch a bus and be along the A4 and back in Reading in a couple of hours - a weird thought when we compared it to our ten days' walking under the high wide sky of the Ridgeway. Two different levels of time. We think the world is small because we have shrunk it with motors but when you walk everywhere the land is absolutely fucking immense, seeming endless. Which was just how the Old Ones knew it. A distant ridge, and what lies beyond? And beyond that? The human spirit, ever questing.

Home to the tent struggle splish splosh splash silage water mud bramble-snag nettle woods thank you for letting us find the tent in the wet black dark. Sang stupidly like lost drunken souls and went to sleep.

2022

Madhead: What an adventure. Was I there?

I remember the Ridgeway Café bit (probably because of the photos) and the Bell Inn bit because it was such a dire place. Didn't we eat out in style on our dwindling holiday money! As with yesterday's comment, I don't remember the rain. It must have rained because the diary says it did. Short-term memory loss is one thing but LONG-term memory loss is, is, um ... Oh look! Our snowdrops are out!

The decision to not get the bus home couldn't have taken long to make. By then we were committed pilgrims; especially as we'd just weathered the weather. Which I don't remember. Did I already say?

Roger: Sometimes I smile my hello when passing the expensively well-equipped head to toe over 60s walkers striding purposefully with their lightweight ergonomic walking poles, chins pointing to the rest of their perfect retirement, and I think - I do it this way, scruff jacket. Isn't that a sweet thought? We're all specks on trails living our little lives. Those Chinese inkbrush paintings: huge mountain landscapes, with tiny figures making their way along trails.

'...like everybody everywhere we didn't put on our waterproof jackets until we were already wet'

Zen homework: study this statement deeply.

I remember this day and the discomfort, staring at the ground passing below my eyes, each mile the longest mile of the walk so far, rain beat face. Unfamiliar with acts of endurance, me a hippie weed! Expert at avoiding the rugby scrum and knowing the short cuts on cross country runs at school. But here discovering that feeling that goes with endurance. Looking up and out and there's the amazing breathtaking vast sweep of the land down from the Ridgeway. Mile after mile until…

THE RIDGEWAY CAFÉ! The most sacred site of all! Entering the steamy window'd hall of hot greasy food, mugs of tea, music pound from juke box! Resting the aching legs and removing the digging straps. Can I see the nurse, please? Food on a thing called plate.

Then after our all too brief sojourn in heaven - out into drizzle. After the café, a homeless feeling. This is why they invented the house. Muscles: no! no! no! You're making a mistake! When you're soaked wet through and the process of evolution is reversing back to amoeba, you might as well just lie in a ditch and give way to it, become one with soggy, but we made the effort. It was like there actually wasn't anywhere to camp so we had to find some sort of clearing in the foot snaring brambles in an unwelcoming wood. Pitch tent and just sit in it. Nope. Pub and the five-pint cure? Yes. Then sleep like a damp log with all the other damp logs.

Squash: I don't think I have ever fully dried out.

A drying out day and a thorough airing in wonderful sunny Avebury

From the diary:

Wake up WET. Everything is in various degrees of wet from damp to wringing. The woods are drenched, vegetation drooping with water. No fire last night. No fire this morning. Can see how crucial to well-being a fire must have been for our distant ancestors, they must've loved the first cave-dweller who invented a box of matches. Packed up carelessly, everything rolled, squished and bundled up, and slopped back along the A4 road to the Ridgeway Cafe on Overton Hill for another delightful dose of egg chippy bean.

We took a walk down to West Kennet Long Barrow, a place we had visited and enjoyed omming and chanting in last year during Our Cosmic Capers Club outing, before making our way back across the main road towards Avebury. Clouds slowly dispersing as we procession along West Kennet Stone Avenue, ancient stones pointing the way and stirring deep muddy questions about what the Old Ones knew that we don't know.

Some warmth on our backs and the grass sprinkled with beautiful shiny golden buttercups in which I would live in gold were I a flower elf. Talked to some bullocks who licked our hands roughly with their monster cats' tongues then into the vast Avebury Henge to lean on a stone, spread out our wetlings around to dry and hang out the unwashed washing, bringing a common touch to the living stones. Those big old stones hold a lot of heat, our dossbags steaming nicely in the warming noontime. Casually watch a freak with his hand up his lady's jumper and write some more of this sometimes tiresome diary. Fagtime in the sun. Lay the tent out to dry and consider the fate of a redface sleeping drunk, bombed out on cider, the bottle by his side, and his soon to be poor aching head. We wanted to stay in Avebury so hunted round for a place to camp - but it wouldn't feel right, somehow sacrilegious, to doss within the great circles or ditches.

A Mr Laley suggested a treed triangle of open grass next to a housing estate at Avebury Trusloe, a lane's walk north-west from the stones: said we could probably camp there. We had a gander but we were paranoid about all the kids milling around so we went back to the village and knocked on some doors asking other people if they had some land to camp on. Most turned us away but the folks in a big old house on the Swindon Road wanted to charge us 75p to camp in their massive garden (that's about £15 in today's money).

By now I'm getting bolshy. Don't these fuckers realise that we are holy men on an aimless quest for something we don't know the name of? I got a big pain in the guts from all the bollocks and bullshit but eventually our karma and destiny led us back to Avebury Trusloe: we threw the tent up and it was cool, the local kids all buzzing around were nice, excited by our weird presence, and full of questions. We gave them strange mystical answers. This little council estate, as usual plonked some distance from the "proper people", was neat and tidy, like Emmer Green where I grew up, populated with decent people bringing up their families. Some of the mums came down to the tent to check us out, interviewed us. We gave them slightly less strange mystical answers, and they seemed ok with it. The kids were on half-term I think and they hung around till dark, till called home for tea and bed. They collected up some firewood for us and sat round the fire. It was nice to be dry again and eat some billy-can boilings.

2022

Madhead: At last I remember the damp bit. The drying out with the help of ancient stone magic and copious sunshine is much less of a distant memory. I got the feeling that I could stay there for ever. At that time there was a grocer's shop, a butcher, and a pub so it seemed like a good prospect. Don't know how I would have made any money though. Fifty years ago there wouldn't have been much scope for a printer in a village.

As for where we camped I think that, despite our wild *desperado* appearance, what saved us from being hassled and/or firebombed was the fact that we were three in a tent, and with booted feet instead of a van. They had obviously realised that we weren't "casing their joints" if that's still the correct thievery vernacular.

Roger: The sun came out after our trial and initiation by soaking and I remember feeling a different kind of reverence and respect for these huge stones as we walked between them down to the Avebury circle, where it felt OK to drape our wet clothes, bedding and tent over them and take our rest.

After a rest we searched and eventually found our pitch next to the council houses where we received approval from the children who became our companions, sharing our fireside sometimes and listening to our stories. It made me feel like we were nomads in a window of time when travellers were respected and acted respectfully.

That was all we wanted really, we were living a dream in a window of time, in touch with something that could never last, that felt almost lost.

Squash: That little council estate at Avebury Trusloe was, in the end, one of the greatest finds of the walk. For one thing it reminded me of the council estate where I grew up, all tidy and full of purpose, busy with the daily moil and toil and joy of raising families in the maelstrom of life's demands. Crowds of excitable hollering kids running free as nature intended, boys and girls together, as nature intended, visited by fascinating strangers as nature intended, bringing strange news from afar. I liked that we were checked out by a posse of mums and passed whatever test it was that we were examined for. The kids were instructed not to annoy the gentlemen and then left to do their worst. Hahaha. I suppose we kept the little darlings out of the house and out from under feet. Of dads we saw nothing. It was a blessed spot that made us feel welcome and noble. It also made me realise that the life of the village of Avebury was so much more immediate, pressing and vital than the silent sentinels of the ancient standing stones which belonged to other immediate, pressing and vital communities that were now remote and lost in the distant past, whatever magic we invest in them. Life is for those who live.

It's our delight on a Friday night

This is Friday, we're camped just outside Avebury next to the little housing estate at Avebury Trusloe, and we're expecting weekend guests to our commodious dwelling tonight, courtesy of the Post Office delivering our postcards. Better than email, just a little slower. I was wrong yesterday about the kids round here being on half-term, there's no sign of them today, not until the late afternoon when they appeared in their gleeful hordes.

Warning – there are some yesteryear turns of phrase in this entry.

From the diary this day, dot dot dottety dot ... read on ...

Breakfast was sworn-at porridge with innocent unabused raisins. Sunshine, proper summer sunshine at last, lovely Avebury. Dug out the Indian cheesecloth shirts from the scrunched up mess at the bottom of our rucksacks. Nice breezy freedom to wear and I can see Madhead's nipples. We walked down this nice blossomy lane, crossed the little bridge over the stream that demarcates middle-class Avebury Village from the peasantry beyond, up the lovely main street, past the church and squatted in the sun by the wall of the tiny car-park. We made good use of the public bogs to take our ease on a seat for once and to have a good wash in the cold water basin.

Visited the Alexander Keiller Museum behind the church – the kindly keen curator dug us digging love and ley-lines and the ancient sites of the Old Ones. Madhead was excitedly zapped by exhibits of stone phalli and fossilised dog excreta. We all laughed at the official booklet on Avebury and Stonehenge that depicted images of primitive hairy old cavemen with their arses hanging out as the builders of these fantastical places. No cavewomen to be seen. Didn't they know that, in evolutionary terms the people then were exactly the same Homo saps as the people now? Yer custodian man was touchy-feelingly friendly, think he might be queer, seemed to fancy one or all of us but mostly Madhead.

Went in the church for something to do. I don't like churches, never have, but the history of these places gets to you, sitting bold and commanding in their parishes. Come to think of it I've never liked Christianity either, a miserable, gloomy, death-dealing religion that glorifies suffering and wields it to keep the dispossessed in fear and obedience. Such a weird contrast to the image I have of Jesus with the sunshine in him and kindly blessings of love flying out of him in all directions to anyone and everyone. There's a mystery. This church is made nicer by an ornate painted rood loft which (I read) was hidden, on pain of death, from that miserable warty bastard Cromwell behind a lath and plaster wall – and was rediscovered in 1870 something and re-erected.

Went back to the camp for my jacket and discovered a short cut across a field. Getting to groove on spacey Avebury people - into Mr Perry's shop and the butcher's shop and had a picnic of cheese, bread, pickled onions, Blackthorn Cider, mushrooms and a banana. Glub. Learnt from Mr Perry that there was once a lot more cottages inside the henge but Alexander Keiller bought and demolished some of them and that this fanatical policy was continued by the National Trust in cohorts with the Ministry of Public Buildings and Works - to buy them when they came up for sale and remove them - with the aim of returning the stone circle to some imaginary former state. This shocked and agitated me. The village is great, full of life and people and the National fucking Trust wants to destroy it for the sterile sake of stones that the Old Ones put up for reasons we no longer understand. The great thing about Avebury is that the magnificent henge and ditches are incidental – they are just sort of there, in and around the village, doing whatever it is they do, which is how I like the manifestations of the past, rather than being museumified like a dead exhibit. I reckon the stones warm to the sounds of playing shrieking children. Surprised to discover that I would keep the village and sacrifice the stones if shit came to shove.

Fell asleep on the grass ruminating on these and other things, woke up and admired a chick with nice stand-up tits. Met some freaks from Essex, got stoned with them, got zipped zapped blapped met Rick who is visiting us from Wokingham, waited around for Russ to also arrive, went to the camp and Russ turned up from Bath with Susie and another guy called Roger (who I will call Roger Man II) and some food, lovely food, what a treat. They and Rick went to Silbury Hill for the sunset. Later we cooked feasted wined and smoked with all the little kids running around or sitting by the fire, allowed up late I think, no school tomorrow. They peeled off in ones and twos to beddy-byes and we sat around poking the fire with sticks while Russ told stories nice. They left late, we retired replete.

2022

Madhead: It was great to have guests; especially when they brought all that food! And, with the greatest respect to Squash and Roger, it was a real treat to be able to talk to somebody else for a change. A bit like being astronauts in a space station and enduring radio silence for 11 days until mission control fixed the comms.

Roger: I like what you said about the stones and the village, Squash. There's warmth, the people living among the stones. The sound of playing children, warming the stones. Stones listening and looking back with big stone faces.

looking at a stone, touching a stone
hand flat on warm stone face
gritty feel on palm

It's been a long time now since we walked together,
dinner from the billycan, fireside talking

and when we were there it had been a long time
since the folk of the stones did what they did,
whatever that was.

I don't quite know what the feeling is
but I like it that way
a kind of old feeling, deep feeling.
I feel all sad or something but it's a good feeling.

Squash: It was quite the little party we had, ornamented with excited children and types of food we'd forgotten about. I wonder who Roger Man II was. I wondered why he stayed in the camp with us when Russ and Susie went home. I forgot to ask but they probably didn't know him either. I expect he was a hitch-hiker they picked up. Seemed like a nice fellow anyway.

Avebury is just great, the way it enfolds you in its bizarre yet mellow combination of the ancient stones – just a'happening to be there – and the village life going on all around. I like the idea of the bus pulling in and the driver shouting "anyone for the Neolithic or the Bronze Age. Better get on board now, we are about to depart … this bus is 5,000 years late". Hahaha.

The day after the night before

From dat ole scruffy diary for this Saturday:

No longer having to know what day it is, it's amazing that you could still tell it was a Saturday right from the moment of waking up. A different vibe. I always thought, when I was a kid, that Saturdays were yellow and this one was as yellow as the cowslips. With Madhead and Rick we sauntered down the sunny flowery lane into the village to the little butcher's-cum-grocery in a side road to buy oats for breakfast. It is one of those shops that has just one or two packets of each thing displayed on the shelf with big spaces between them. We had to buy Weetabix as the lady shopkeeper had no porridge oats. After we paid, and seeing our disappointment, she told us to wait and went out back to her kitchen and returned with half a packet of her own oats which she laid on us, with a great big beaming smile. How nice, our simple, but bewildering, mission is being met with such kindness.

So, back at the camp, we all guzzled Weetabix with thick gold top milk we got from the milkman. Spent some time chatting with all these sweet kids that were buzzing around like hoverflies - Theresa, Tracy, Graham, David, Stuart - who wanted to know "what you doing today then?" We said we had things to do and split. Also split sometime in the night was Roger Man II who left a scribbled note "I have left early as is my wont. Thank you for food and shelter which I was in need of. Here's a little cash, not for payment, but as a gift towards your journey". That was nice, we're 40p richer (about £5 in today's money). I wonder who he was.

We walked over fields to Windmill Hill having read in the Museum about the Beaker People, an immigration of white-skinned, blue-eyed folk with new advanced technologies. Beakers mostly, hahaha. These people apparently totally displaced the indigenous Neolithic farmers across the whole of Britain. Makes you wonder what powerful stuff they had in their beakers. Rick and Madhead had dropped a tab of acid each and were tripping. It was really hot. Got sunburnt. I expected something powerful from Windmill Hill but it was kind of hard to see it and feel it. Then we went to and scrambled up to the top of Silbury Hill, great views from up there. Trying to imagine it shining across the landscape, all gleaming white chalk, with its deep deep ditch around it. Whatever drove the Old Ones to all this effort was a powerful force indeed, informed by a knowledge, or a belief system, that we can only puzzle over. Just imagine it struck by moonbeams in the dark silent land thousands of years ago. You'd gasp and gape for sure.

Tumbled back down and into the Silbury Café, nestled in the small car-park near the mound's foot, for strangely acid-inflected tea and cakes experience, everyone feeling weird, nervy laughter and awkward ejaculations you get being close to people flying, the non-trippers resonating with whatever is beaming from the round black spinning eyeballs of the acid spacemen.

Back across the fields I went into Avebury for groceries. Got into a mouth trip, feeling the world on lip tooth tongue and gum, singing Roger's comical version of that lounge-lizard Sinatra song "It's the Good Life, lots of luvverly things to put in my mouth" Back later for playing with dem kids and making dinner - boiled rice, onions and potatoes, lentils, hiziki seaweed, brown bread and miso. Had a big sing-song round the fire and looned around, the kids slowly fading away one by one into the growing night. Glad mad and tired and pleased that I have brought the diary up to date again after the visitors.

Madhead: Did the butcher give us a bag of pinhead oatmeal or do I imagine this? If he did, then he was a very kind man. With one or two exceptions, as were all of the people we encountered on our ramble. If we'd been cyclists, however, it would have been a different thing altogether. Nobody seems to like cyclists.

I seem to recollect that Rick and I shared the tab of acid. And I also believe (I stand to be corrected) that was the last time I ever took acid. It was going out of fashion towards things like speed which was probably easier to manufacture but wasn't a thing I thought I might enjoy.

Silbury Hill is one of the most remarkable places on the planet. Was it an ancient British equivalent of the Tower of Babel? Maybe an early warning weather station? Who can say? To us it's just there. Built by sheer effort for just the hell of it, probably.

Those kids are now in their late fifties. Do you think they ever think of us and recount their childhood memories at dinner parties? No. I don't think so either.

Fun fact for pub quiz fans: *It's the Good Life* was by Tony Bennett, aka Anthony Dominick Benedetto. A different, but strangely similar, lounge lizard.

Roger: Three or four years after our walk I'm at art college in London attending a lecture by Michael Dames who'd just published his book, The Silbury Treasure. He presented a very convincing vision of Silbury Hill being part of a massive earthwork artwork, the hill being the pregnant womb of the Earth Mother, rising from the surrounding tremendous moat that formed, from above, her reclining body. At her vagina, the source of the River Kennet previously known as Cunnit, the name of a fertility goddess, says he.

Having to be "convinced" about "theories" has never bothered me, but it was a neck hair raising afternoon of storytelling archaeologicalness which took me back to our humble wandering along the sweeping curves of Mother earth.

A Saturday as yellow as corn, blessed with golden sun. I reckon the beaming lady of kindness in the shop must have been Ceres the goddess of grain, and the milkman bearing gold top milk must have been a milkman.

Squash: I'm sure it was the butcher's wife who gave us her own oatmeal from her kitchen. She was lovely and very clean. She had on a shopkeeper's apron which I liked.

I stand corrected – it was Tony Bennett as Madhead says. All those post-war swooning crooners sounded and seemed the same to me. Smooth, unctuous sexual predators.

I bumped into one of those merry Trusloe boys many years later in Avebury. It was Stuart, the one Madhead carried around on his shoulders, and he hailed me "excuse me, are you Squash?" and it turned out I was, even though I was wearing a different head by then. What a nice young man he was, probably in his early twenties, maybe the same age we were on the Walk. He said our arrival and presence was one of the highlights of his childhood and how mystified and disappointed he was when we disappeared. What goes around comes around.

We were very much in touch with the sweeping curves of Mother Earth but we never made it to the vagina. Not then anyway.

And yes, I also believe the milkman was some kind of milkman.

Vanishing into the night

On this Sunday from the diary (which incidentally is falling to bits having lain undisturbed for 40 odd years):

Breakfast of Weetabix with nuts and raisins. The local Halflings were up before us and hovering around the tent and chattering when we woke up. Went into the village with the pesky kids, giving them what they called "chuggies" - piggy-backs and shoulder-carries.

They have shown us the quick route across a field, like kids everywhere they know their way around their neighbourhood better than adults. Went in the public bog and washed face, hands and shirt in cold water and a bar of that hard green soap beloved of grannies. Met some freaks in the south-west corner of the stones. The kids were onto us to see "their" tunnel at the bottom of Green Street (also known as The Herepath) which leads up to the Downs and the Ridgeway. This was the street in the village where cottages had been demolished by The Ministry of Works and the National Trust in the late 1940s and 50s. The tunnel was narrow, dark, damp and long, went right under the bank with the beech trees above, their roots grasping the soil of the bank like the bony hands of a crone. No idea what the tunnel was, or what it was for, maybe an old badger sett or someone mining the chalk out … Just another mystery in this most mysterious of places.

We eventually managed to shake the kids off - they didn't dig it, wanted to stay with us for the day - and walked up the track to the edge of the Downs and a Nature Conservancy area where the Grey Wethers sunbathe - big old stones scattered around on the hilltop. These are the same kind of stones that made the standing mono-liths in the Avebury Henge and the sarsen stones from the Marlborough Downs at Stonehenge. It makes me laugh when the experts talk about these stones being brought from "nearby" compared to the bluestones at Stonehenge brought all the way from the Preseli Mountains in Wales. The amount of effort it must've taken to shift just one of these monsters a hundred yards defies belief.

"Come on lads, we've got to shift a few of these right down there, better get on with it."

"Are you fucking joking man?"

I wonder wonder wonder what they were up to. They clearly had a well above subsis-tence living to have all this free time to piss around humping bloody great stones about and then standing them upright. Hahaha, the things we will never know.

Rick was being really weird, sort of mentally jumpy, twitchy, clumsy and awkward and out of tune with the three of us, and a general bring-down and annoyance like a persistent wasp. Maybe yesterday's acid trip has left him on edge. Or perhaps it's us, having slowed down during our fortnight of simple living out of doors. Dug watching the cattle move across the field of the Grey Wethers, all open strange tracks, trees, rough grass, this herd moving like in a wildlife film of Africa, keeping a wary eye on us and us on them as they drift through the scene. We stopped at a wood. Roger went off to meditate, me Madhead and Rick sitting in the field. Eventually wandered back into Avebury which was full oh so full of tourists enjoying a little Sunday "run out in the car".

Stopped in Mr Perry's shop for cheese and biscuits which we ate by a stone. Then there was a big scene with Ricky and his frustrated head about what he's trying to do and what he's not doing and what he wants to do all spilling out of him. Seems to think everything he's feeling is the world's fault. He was getting on my fucking nerves, so self-absorbed and obviously struggling with something titanic inside that was blinding him to the sunshine, joy and magic all around and the laughter that would be here if he wasn't. I think I said he should maybe get his head out of his arse and breathe the universe for a while. Impatient and unkind of me but this eruption seemed to clear the air a bit.

Madhead, Roger and I went to the vicarage where they were serving tea and scones in the back garden. There was a lovely girl in there, reminded me with a sharp pang of the lately forgotten pleasures of the flesh. This little tea party went a bit crazy: it was such an unlikely collision of middle-England politeness and bizarro weirdo freakvibe that we started acting up and Madhead nearly burst with a monster giggling jag.

Look away dear, don't encourage them.

Later Madhead went back to the camp to fix the grits while we sat in the Lych Gate.

Someone decided we might as well go to the church service, so Roger, Rick and I joined the congregation. So boring. The vicar's wife is no organist and vicar sang the hymns in such a madly high key that no-one could sing along with him with his clever complicated phrasing. Even vicars show off. The sermon was worth a listen, in parts, though. Those kids, David and Stuart, were outside yelling our names. We could hear them halfway through the service "Squash! Squash! Roger! Madhead!" and they ambushed us when we emerged, so we had to chuggy them back to the camp.

Madhead had prepared a dinner of egg fried rice and miso vegetable stew. We sang a few songs and turned in for the night but not before I had another scene with Rick about him not doing any work - collecting firewood, fetching water, cooking, cleaning up, anything - lazy bastard, acting like the world owed him something. Only child syndrome. It's odd because he is a sweet guy really, just helplessly tangled in his own internal dialogue.

Tried to crash out but couldn't sleep, head whirring. Suddenly I heard my mouth say we should pack up and split. Hahaha. It was about 11 o'clock. We thought it would be a great puzzle for the kids to find us disappeared without a trace in the morning, like we never were there. So we fix some cheese and bread to take with us. Rick pitched out into the night, presumably to hitch home or somewhere on his road to something else. Cleared the camp and left it pristine. Us three gliding through silent stone dark Avebury midnight, catching a glimpse of a ghostly apparition of a man with a dim lantern. Pooka-pooka night. Drifted down the stone avenue, through West and East Kennet villages and vanished in the night quiet towards Boreham Wood.

2022

Madhead: The vicarage "tea party" was so weird. I still haven't got over it really. It's burned into my psyche indelibly. I could imagine a white rabbit turning up at any moment.

Parting from Avebury was such sweet sorrow, but it had to be done. It's as if the place was getting a bit fed up with us and was showing us the door. To me, the midnight flit became cathartic as we wandered off under the stars into our next chapter.

Those hippies eh? Never there when you want one.

In hindsight, it was obvious that Rick was a troubled soul and I wish we'd been kinder to him. Having once had ownership of the black dog for a while, I can now understand what must have been going on in his head. Poor Rick, bless him.

I still miss Rick.

Roger: My memory is like a falling to bits diary. The only tattered page I have of this entire day, helped by the photos I took, is sitting at that table in the vicar's tea garden. To have tea and scones at the vicarage was something we, or maybe I, simply couldn't pass up. We knew there was a surreal risk involved. There were guests at the other tables wearing casual Sunday clothes that looked (guests and clothes) like they had been ironed that morning. The soft chink of the china cup. The little pot of strawberry jam. The little pot of butter. Look, a *tablecloth*. We took our places. The lovely girl served us with a smile. We were on our best behaviour. The urge to misbehave was overwhelming. The task of preparing our scones (spoon for jam) and pouring our tea (cup onto saucer then tea poured from pot) required interaction and we started talking in squeaky poopy-doo voices, potentially uncontrollable laughter started to erupt. We were trying not to be too disruptive, which would have been rude, but of course that made matters worse.

I think Madhead was the worst affected, he had to grasp his right arm with his left hand and squeeze very tightly while rocking from side to side, and presumably me and Squash had our own coping strategies to avoid rolling around on the lawn.

Afterwards, as our chronicler records, Madhead went off to reintegrate and cook grub and we sat in the Lych Gate of the church, where a service was about to begin. Going to a church service was something we, or maybe I, simply couldn't pass up.... etc etc

Apart from that:

Thinking about these astonishing feats of stone dragging and landscape carving that left us these places to wonder at, and wander through.

Thinking about our own wandering and sense of wonder that's at the heart of this tale; passing through such places, living simply and leaving no trace.

Thinking about those kids from the council houses who liked us being around and then we just disappeared in the night.

Thinking about Rick walking off into the night on his own.

Squash: The tea party was great, I couldn't have been happier. It seemed like our bounden duty to attend and to spread loveliness far and wide. Why should a tea party be constrained by formality? The ingredients for perfect happiness were there in abundance: sunshine, birdsong, tablecloths, beautiful handmaidens, cake and tea and scones and butter and jam, half-crazed beloved hippy friends and an endless trek stretching out before us.

I was fairly horrible to Rick I think. I had no time for the self-doubt that had doubled back into him and manifested itself in complete oblivion to all the joyful life dancing around him. I couldn't indulge his feelings, just thought he was self-obsessed. Should've been kinder I guess but I'm not sure it would have made any difference. In my own blunt way I was trying to shake him out of the doldrums, blow a gusty wind his way, tell it like it is. It's all sad now, looking back, but he chose and took his own road out of it anyway.

Floating away from Avebury into the silent night was quietly exciting and eerily unearthly.

PART II

Avebury to Stonehenge

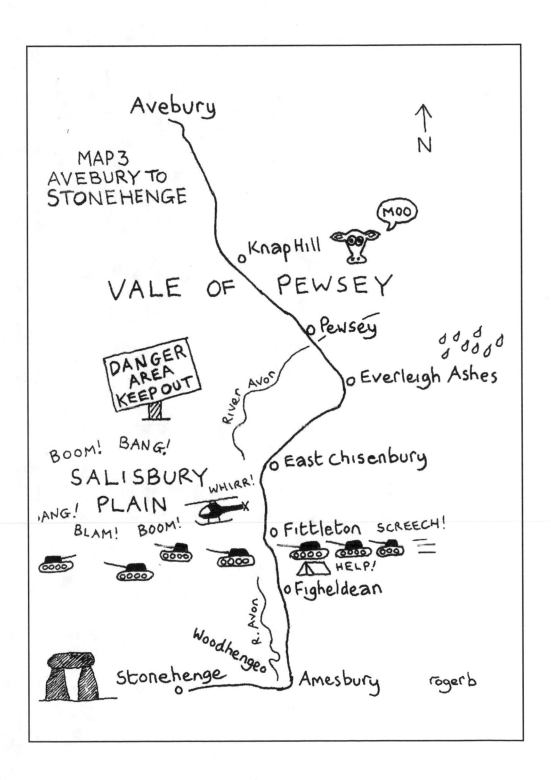

From high night to low valley

The leaving of Avebury marked the end of phase 1 of the Walk, the end of the Ridgeway and the high ancient places for a while. For want of a direct hilltop route to Stonehenge, because of military occupation, we are obliged to meander through the byways of deep England in all its picturesque sniffiness and complex hierarchies. We feel as though we are forced into the Vale of Pewsey, as if the land is pushing us down into the valley and offering few pathways over the hills.

The diary records on this gloomy day:

We walked on through the silent secret night heading south but wanting to go south-west in an eerie night-time light spreading with Venus low above the ridge to our left, clouds clearing, nice star show. Later, the dim grey of a weird false dawn in the east. Presently a crescent moon appears and the birds start singing an hour before sun up. We had decided to go to Glastonbury via Stonehenge and ideally would've gone across Salisbury Plain with all its Neolithic remains to visit and gawp at but the British army seems to have requisitioned virtually all of it and littered it with unexploded ordnance and piss-off signs. There is also our perpetual need to be within reach of civilisation so we can get water and to be close to trees to find fuel for our campfire. So we are forced to find a route on the map which is on old tracks, footpaths and bridleways - anything to avoid the roads - which will take us in the right general direction while hopping from wood to wood.

Tired struggle up to Knap Hill camp where we lay down in our doss bags and fall asleep so quickly that we miss the real dawn. Woken up at 7.15 by Roger nudging me gently and hiss-whispering that we'd better move. I look up and see we are surrounded by cattle leaning over us, all staring, snorting and slobbering what you up to what you doing here so we cautiously pack up and creep away, no sudden movements. I hate to admit that I'm quite scared of cows, their unpredictability mostly, especially in the early summer before the heat's drowsiness quietens them down.

Very tired, it's now overcast, cold and a little rain, stiff legs, stiff mind. Take a so-called bridleway which is heavily overgrown with nettles and cow parsley. A mile through this and we are drenched up the legs, water splashing out of Madhead's boots with each step. Take the road through Wilcot Green past Oak Farm. Stand on the bridge overlooking the still water canal. Quiet dark morning. Stop in woods, reminiscent of Woolstone Dell. Beeches and elms. Starts belting down with rain. Roger goes to the large house on the crossroads for water. Comes back eventually with the big bottle full and the gift of six eggs. A brigadier and his wife overflowing with kindness apparently. Just goes to show.

Eat boiled eggs and bread in the rain. Another soaking. Stoke up the fire for tea and a drying out. A dreary walk into dreary Pewsey. Stopped at a pub for tobacco and a pint. Pub full of Bank Holiday Monday drinkers, friendly enough piss-taking out of us. Must be great being part of some conforming majority to feel entitled to take the piss out of anyone different. Through Pewsey, resting at beautiful St John the Baptist church.

From Pewsey we take a track past a faded hillside White Horse on a very steep struggle hill, braving the frisky cattle for quickness and directness of route. This white horse was carved into the hillside in 1937 and is a poor sort of thing fenced round and without soul or mystique. Onto a long straight high road, swept with drizzle, wrapped in grey cloud. Stopped at a barn wonderfully warm dry sitting on straw. Oh well up we get very tired down the road to house. No answer at the door. Next door, no answer, but keys in the door. Roger and Madhead turn to walk away but I push the door open, go in to the kitchen to get water anyway but hearing a radio I knock on an inside door. A lady comes out from her lounge, gives me water, doesn't even look surprised. Down the road to Everleigh Ashes. Another soaking through the woods but we find a place for camp, quite pleasant. Loads of snares in here, Roger caught his foot in one. We spoil all the snares we see.

Build a fire for good amazing thick sweet porridge with raisins and so zombie to bed like we'd dropped a couple of Mandrax at 5.30 pm.

2022

Madhead: It's the kindness of others that always astonishes me. If anyone was to be foolhardy enough to do the same journey nowadays, I don't doubt that they would have similar experiences. Most people will give you water if you ask, and very often offer substantially more. Regular pub-goers will always take the piss out of strangers, particularly with strange strangers. We were used to it though. The only difference today would be the campfires. Anyone trying that these days would probably be frowned upon.

We were often sleep deprived and weary when we did the daily strike camp, walk for miles, find a camp, collect firewood, erect the tent routine. I think that was one of the reasons we stayed in Avebury for so long.

The Vale of Pewsey felt to me like we were going through a long green tunnel. The wide views from the ridge suddenly were all cut off and only the way forward had any kind of promise and light. Pleasant enough, though. Like walking in a giant's shrubbery.

Roger: Our night time flit was appropriate to the change of feeling as we entered a different landscape and territory. Planning a careful route to avoid theatres of war, stitching old pathways back together with our footsteps, breaking cover to reach the next sanctuary of woodland where we might feel more at home. A different shade of adventure. Part pilgrim, part vagrant.

Those cows, the ground telling the sleeping me of movement on the earth, then jostling snorting above, my eyes bleary open to gigantic cow faces, huge snotwet nostrils and tongues. Driven from Knap Hill Camp by bovine bailiffs.

I can just about remember the jolly brigadier and his wife, or have a sense of them. Comfortably retired, and a glint of adventure as I told them of our journey. I had a feeling they wanted to join us really.

Never one to flinch at a perceived risk of confrontation or making someone jump, Squash walks through another unanswered door, and of course it's OK, just another wild man asking for water.

Then, a wood with snares, and one of them got me. Lucky I wasn't a rabbit. Anyway, an opportunity for some kind-hearted sabotage.

Squash: Pushing at doors, open or shut, seems to have been a lifelong hobby of mine. You never know what might be behind but I had little fear in those days. Now I'm more content to leave whatever lies beyond as a mystery.

Rain stops play

A dismal Tuesday of endless rain spent mostly in the sopping wet woods of Everleigh Ashes. Followers of this expedition will be thrilled to learn that this is the shortest diary entry yet.

Dull diary:

Rained in the night, softly thrumming the tent. Wake up after enormous good sleep. Fire in the rain. Japanese breakfast of onions, potatoes, lentils, green peppers, buckwheat, masses of miso, lashings of tea.

Starts to rain again. Drink tea in the tent and write diary, occasionally peering out through the trees. Hard in the woods to tell if it's still raining. It is. Or is it? Rain on-off. Walk into Everleigh via two damp straight empty roads that could be ley lines or drove roads or both, or neither, to Everleigh Post Office and shop for stamps and provisions.

Back to camp, write long senseless letters to our friends in the Cosmic Capers Club and to our parents. Dear Mum I'm drowning, please send lifeboat. It rains and rains and rains and rains. Tea of Bisk-o-Weet which is some sort of poor man's Weetabix, found only in village stores that have stock that's been hanging about since the 1950s. Rains. Get into the tent. Rains. Let's eat something. Rains. No fire now. Rains. Cheese and bread and peanut butter and Marmite and apple. Rains. Get in the sleeping bags. Rain coming in the seams of the tent. Get out of the sleeping bag and out of the tent for a piss. Rains.

We talk about weird acid trip scenarios we've been into and out of, this talk giving us mild flashbacks and LSD dry mouth and throat. Rains. Give up and go to bed. Already in bed. Rains. We don't mind too much. We're in the woods.

Madhead: Dull day indeed. Fifty years on and we'd have been playing Candycrush and looking at Facebook or sexting on our phones all day. Assuming we had solar. And a signal. Instead, we talked a lot, wrote letters and generally looned about, weather permitting.

There was always a need for fire though and when there wasn't one life became troublesome for me. I suppose it's the home and hearth thing – comfort and ease at the end of the day. I don't recall many days when it was too wet for a fire of some sort.

In fact it's a similar day outside today, although it's February and therefore windy too, so I'm now off to light the woodburner and pour myself an ample drop of scotch. Bliss.

Roger: That Japanese breakfast sounds good

We've a good supply of miso, it's there in every meal.

I must get some miso

I miss miso so

Squash: Every so often the universe dishes up a dank Tuesday. Better to be in a tent in the wet woods than not in a tent in the wet woods. I remember it quite fondly because the rain was so insistent there was no choice but to "stay in" and play house. Hahaha, like a little happy family of vagrants put on pause and sustained by miso.

Playing with the army

After yesterday's sustained soaking this Wednesday sees our intrepid wanderers out and about again, shaking off the raindrops and fluffing up their fur. Your reporter has some kind of philosophical head-fit and premonition about future memories.

From the diary:

Build good roaring fire to dry everything out. Still squally and overcast but we're hopeful of it clearing up. Breakfast of Bisk-O-Weet and raisins and walnuts. We pack up, drying the tent thoroughly first. Split Everleigh Ashes about 11.30.

We've decided to turn west as Sidbury Hill, the way we wanted to go, is closed for army manoeuvres. It seems like everything around here is controlled or affected by the military. A short-cut through a field gets us drenched again, along a track and out onto the main Andover-Devizes road. It's pretty dismal walking along main roads but it's only a couple of miles. The road goes through the RAF camp, high fences topped with barbed wire, military regulation-length lawn, get your flaming hair cut you horrible little man. The whole armed forces thing is a bizarre long-lasting worked-out game with big very expensive toys to play with and ruin and well-paid officer jobs for life for public school thickos. I'm sure there are better things to waste all that money on when people go hungry and poor.

Then we turn south along the line of the River Avon to East Chisenbury. This is a different kind of England from the high ways and ancient tracks. Historic rather than pre-historic. Cosy and settled and buttoned up and buttoned down rather than wild and strange and mystical. The sort of places that raiders in the old times would descend on for a bit of arson, pillage and mayhem which is what I feel like doing.

We see a thatcher at work on one of the cottages and ask him what's behind the common custom hereabouts of putting straw birds on the ridge of thatched roofs.

Amazingly he says he is the very man who started it all about 20 years ago – and only then on the whim of one lady who fancied having a bird on the roof, and the idea catching on so that every job now wants one. Into the Red Lion in East Chisenbury for a welcome pint and later we walk through beautiful quidsy Enford. Much riches in this valley I'd say. We stop outside of Fittleton in a thin beech wood on a bank above a very minor road. Knock up a dinner of potato, carrot, hiziki, onion stew, buckwheat, apple, bread and Marmite.

It seems we've pitched our tent on a bees' nest and they might be a little annoyed. A weird day, distant artillery blamming away on Salisbury Plain conjuring up fantasies of Che Guevara and the woods throwing up images of Robin Hood. It's a bit edgy being a peacefreak in enemy territory.

There's a really friendly cow in the adjacent field, a young Guernsey, or is it a Jersey, beautiful tan hide and gentle face, nice change from unruly Friesians, perfect cow for a friendly freaky farm. We moved the tent to a lumpy place so the bees could have their space back.

We had a rap about money again and how little we had of it and decided that peckish pecks are out, fags are an unaffordable luxury, eat more rice, less vegetables. Cut our expenses, cut out beer. Boo-hoo. Roger has been singing amazing songs of when the world was young full of mystery and magic as indeed it still is if you are.

Sings:
It was pleasant and delightful on a midsummer morn
And the green fields and the meadows were all covered in corn
The blackbirds and thrushes sang on every green spray
And the lark she sang melodious at the dawning of the day

Chorus:
And the lark she sang melodious
And the lark she sang melodious
And the lark she sang melodious
At the dawning of the day.

Three travellers digging the one and the several. Getting in tune with the all-around and the inside of things – learning the gentle way, slow ways, thoughts and feelings ebb and flow like the tides of the sea, sway like the trees in the breeze. We could be the last generation to be able to do this as selfish territorial ownership nibbles away at all the overlooked, unkempt and in-between spaces. There's a deep England from long long ago living just over the hedge, unseen and unfelt by the world rushing by. Our friendly cow just looking in on us wondering where the singing's coming from. Please don't eat our guy ropes nice cows.

I experience a sudden upsurge of joy and well-being, washing over me in waves. I'm loving this walk, so many things to say all of a sudden, all my head, all my feelings, all flavour of it to be forgotten like the rest of life's hooks and hitches and nooks and itches but probably to be glimpsed and savoured in the future sometime when a fully rounded fragrant memory comes flitting back to you, taking you by surprise. Ah yes, one day I'll say I remember … Ah the transience! That's what's sad. And beautifully actually inevitably real. All things must pass.

Madhead: Anything to do with militariyness gives me the collywobbles. High razor-wire fences in particular. Were they keeping strangers out or themselves in? They must have been in terror of us free spirits ambling through without a care in the world.

Only halfway to our destination and we realise we don't have enough money for beer. Still, at least we had our health. And singing comes for free.

Thank goodness your diary survived. *Ah yes, one day I'll say I remember ...*

Roger: Military territory has a palpable lifelessness to it. Non-places devoid of soul. Something to do with being ready for warfare or preparing for warfare. The spirits of place shrink away, hibernate, and wait.

Somebody once told me that the fairy tale Sleeping Beauty is an allegory related to the deforestation of Northern Europe. The spirit of the sleeping forest will wake again.

We stay on our side of the barbed wire. Perhaps we should have asked if we could camp in their camp for the night, after all it's a camp. Light a fire and get the billy on the boil. Soldiers joining us like the kids in Avebury did.

We carry on walking from woodland to woodland. The MOD territory we're skirting round in contrast to all that is at the heart of our undefined quest for somethingness.

Squash: Gulp. The military was just about the complete antithesis of us in every respect and we did not feel "at ease" around them. At school when we reached the fifth form we were obliged to join the CCF – the Combined Cadet Force. I refused, said I was a conscientious objector. The school was bewildered, then furious, then capitulated: so while all my fellows were square-bashing and lugging around rifles I was incarcerated under the supervision of a prefect and made to write essays for two hours on inspirational subjects, such as "One square inch of wall", "The head of a drawing pin" or "The death of a moth".

Hahaha, little did they know that I enjoyed writing and that had given my imagination free rein to improvise and explore. I've never really been fond of the armed forces or prefects and other disciplinarians since (or before). Oh well. I know that soldiers are ostensibly there to protect us but I have never felt protected around soldiers. Threatened, yes, protected, no.

An early morning wake-up call, courtesy of the army, fear and loathing, fear of cows transmuting into fear of pennilessness. Another day on and off the road

From the diary this day:

At twenty to one this morning we were startled awake as tanks roared past on the track at the bottom of the bank within feet of the tent. We were all terrified, sounded like they were coming through the tent, ground shaking, trees shaking, everything shaking. Oh fuck, what is happening? It's Armageddon. Jesus. Gone the romantic guerrilla revolution visions of yesterday, in with the horrifying reality of modern machine warfare, the ear-splitting noise, the terror, the hatred, the extreme violence, the despair. Men younger than us grinning confident in their turrets looking forward to testing out their new found expertise somewhere in the world and on some poor bastards for real. And later, in the early morning grey, helicopters flying over from behind, heavy field artillery slamming away in the distance. A taste of what it must've been like in Vietnam behind the lines in comparative safety. As they say, fuck that for a game of soldiers.

Breakfast of porridge, buckwheat and raisins then off we walk back down the valley to Fittleton, stopping at All Saints Church for a rest. The good, best, thing about these churches is that they are always open and you can sit down in the dry, if not the warm, cold Christian charity being what it is. Continue through Netheravon village, now camped outside Figheldean, near the fallen-on-hard-times, crumbling and dishevelled Syrencot House, now a builder's office and yard, and formerly a splendid Georgian mansion.

We got water there and asked for casual work to boost our dwindling funds. No deal, but the guy there was friendly enough, suggested we ask for casual work at farms, which we've decided to try. But remembering my stint at hop-picking in Kent, which turned out to be blackcurrant-picking, I was not so keen. I remember from three years ago, 26 lbs of blackcurrants, NO STALKS OR LEAVES, for £1, bloody hot tedious slave labour it was. It took three of us a day and a half to earn £5 between us.

Now sitting under a splendid copper beech. Army on all sides of us. Low-flying Hawker Hunters splitting the sky overhead, roaring thunder and promising sudden death. Terror from the skies. Feel like renegades or deserters on the lam, trapped in a battleground, crouched in a huddle, wondering what will happen next. I said farewell this morning to the smiling loving Guernsey/Jersey cow – I got in the field with her and spoke to her and stroked her and she was as gentle and affectionate as ever. I don't know why this one was keen to make friends when all the others stayed at a distance but I won't forget her and will be grateful to her for helping me overcome my irrational nervousness of the bovine beasts and their unpredictability.

We fixed our grits for dinner in this fucking mental war-zone. Rice and lentils, sardines, onion, bread. The moment dinner was cooked it pissed down with rain, so we ate in silence in the tent. I always really hated sardines. Now I like sardines. I'd have sardines morning noon and night now. Amazing what famishment can do. It's depressing in this valley, rain coming in the tent again. Even had a game of I-spy, that's how edgy and bored we were. I-spy with my little eye something beginning with H. Helifuckingcopter? Correct.

Roger and I went out midst the splosh to stir the fire into life and make some tea. Madhead came out too and we got a nice rap going about balancing your head out instead of being tossed hither and thither on childish emotions. Nice roaring fire going. Went to bed late but couldn't sleep for a long time with all the pandemonium echoing round my brain.

2022

Madhead: I don't think I have ever been as scared as I was that night. Being that close to tank tracks as to be able to smell the hot grease. Maybe it was my trousers.

At home, here in the wilds of Somerset, we often get processions of helicopters toing and froing between Yeovilton and wherever so I've become quite immune to them. Sometimes, though, they come over so low and loud they rattle the house's very bones. *Then* I notice them, run out into the garden, and shake my fist. It hasn't stopped them yet.

As to casual work, I wonder what we would have been capable of. If anything, we were most qualified to work a treadmill.

Roger: Three Hippies Crushed in Early Hours Tank Horror.

Being woken up like this must have emptied adrenalin glands into our nervous system saved for the worst possible situation. Fight or Flee? Put your knives on lads! Or can three of us run for our lives while still in an orange nylon tent? Seriously thought we'd blown it in choosing where to rest our heads for the night.

But actually, once we'd realized we weren't going to become one with the forest floor, it was an amazing loud and terrifying sight, tanks, armoured cars, field artillery, aerials, blinding lights and we very small three had a literally ringside view of the war machine going off to play pop guns on the plain.

In the morning, porridge, buckwheat and raisins.

And the larks they sang melodious... somewhere else probably.

Yea, that feeling of being a deserter on the run. I used to have a recurring dream in which I'd found myself in the army with different surreal scenarios of sneaking off and avoiding capture. They never caught up with me. That night in the tent it definitely felt like they had.

Squash: For the first time on the Walk I had the feeling of being somewhere I didn't belong, on someone else's patch, on land over which they had complete dominion. To this day I don't know what is wrong with us humans, all this ferocity, all these terrifying weapons, all this effort and enthusiasm for creating mayhem and, let's face it, committing murder. Murder is apparently allowed as long as you obey the rules of war. It's insane. What's the difference between bombing and shelling places where people live (allowed) and randomly shooting civilians (not allowed).

And all this murderous human ferocity is directed at ... who? At us, at humans. Mental. I couldn't wait to get back to the wild places if this is what being civilised meant.

Syrencot House was the secret venue for planning of the Normandy landings,- the listed building description says "the house as a military residence of Lt Gen Browning, General Sir Richard Gale and Lord Allenbrooke, saw the founding of the airborne divisions, and the planning and mounting of Operation Overlord". Churchill was also in attendance and no doubt pissed.

Day 19 Friday 1 June 1973

To the cold winter stones

Finally out of that strange claustrophobic valley this Friday, leaving behind the baffling juxtaposition of chocolate-box villages with their thatched cottages and the brain-thumping militarism of the army all over the Plain. And off to another man-made mystery ...

The diary says:

Well June has at least started bright and sunny. So glad to be out of the depressing Avon valley, we packed up and walked down a footpath to Amesbury. Stopped at the Friar Tuck Cafe which was just like my old rocker haunt, the Viking Café in Reading, for a cup of tea. Did our meagre shopping and ambled west out of town, past the big funfair, to this thin old patch of wooded earthwork, near Amesbury Abbey, a grand Victorian pile built on the site of a former Benedictine abbey of women. This slight earthwork is the remains of an iron-age hillfort with an erroneous Roman name - Vespasian's Camp. Although only a narrow strip of unkempt land near the road it suits us as a camping spot, providing our essential need – firewood. We made our familiar dinner of rice and lentils with potatoes and onions, bashed up with miso paste, bread and cheese.

After feeding ourselves and clearing up we walked slowly towards sunset shiny steely sarsen sombre Stonehenge. Approached from this direction it is picked out against the stormcloud darkening sky, all brooding, ruined and splintered, like broken teeth in a bruised mouth. Ancient stone saxophones, Roger calls them. One good thing is that Roger has produced from somewhere another roll of film for his camera.

There's hardly anyone about. We sit on the fallen stones, touch and stroke the uprights, marvel at the ingenuity and the effort, wonder at the incredible age of it and the meaning of it all. It's such a contrast to the even older monument at Avebury. Where Avebury seems to belong to the summer sunlight and the long days, Stonehenge seems to belong to the dark and the cold and the winter. Avebury embraces, Stonehenge excludes. After a good while we move off, deep in thought, across fields but see in the distance, coming this way, a landowner man with a bang-stick so we hide off down a track that leads towards a lone barrow and the settlement of Lake until he has gone.

Got back to camp, sat around the fire a bit, went to bed. No sleep for ages.

2022

Madhead: The first time I ever went to Stonehenge was on a school trip in 1964. The entrance fee for children was thrupence and the ticket was bought from a little old man in a little wooden hut with a Dutch door and a small countertop across the bottom half of the door. There were postcards for sale, samples of which were pinned to the opened out top half. Nowadays it's a little different -- not exactly Disneyfied, but just as expensive. I always feel a little saddened every time I go near the place these days. They are just a bunch of stones now, accompanied by busfuls of milling crowds hunching over their smartphones. Nothing like the magical times we spent there in our more youthful days.

Amesbury is a lovely place still. Nice medieval street pattern. It was where, in 1964, you could buy *Lady Chatterley's Lover* because it was in Wiltshire and allowed to be on sale but in Berkshire it was still banned. Of course the teacher found out and confiscated all our copies. Authoritarian bastard.

Roger: Not long after we witnessed, hidden by bushes, the ear screeching, ground shaking monster of battlefield weaponry do we find ourselves changing course to avoid an approaching figure ambling along with his shotgun. I don't remember the man with the gun but I can't help putting the two images together.

"I will try to express myself in some mode of life or art as freely as I can and as wholly as I can, using for my defence the only arms I allow myself to use: silence, exile, and cunning" *

The stones of the henge as Squash describes, standing dark and foreboding in the landscape, so different from Avebury. To be able to arrive on foot the way we did is no longer possible, gradually coming closer and closer until that first contact of hand on stone.

* *Portrait of the Artist as a Young Man* – James Joyce

Squash: That was the time to visit Stonehenge: the walk towards it in the gusty, squalling evening bringing a sense of eerie anticipation. Even the dull roar and swish of occasional cars passing on the main road seemed to add to the feeling of remoteness as we first viewed the brooding stones on the darkling plain. There was nothing to bar our way as we entered the henge. I found nothing uplifting about the place but there was an electric sense of awesome latent power as if the stone circle could commune with the sky. The horizon in all directions across the plain showed a narrow band of silver light beneath a sullen black and purple mountain of cloud. It is a place of majesty and mystery and it struck silence into our hearts.

PART III

Stonehenge to King Alfred's Tower

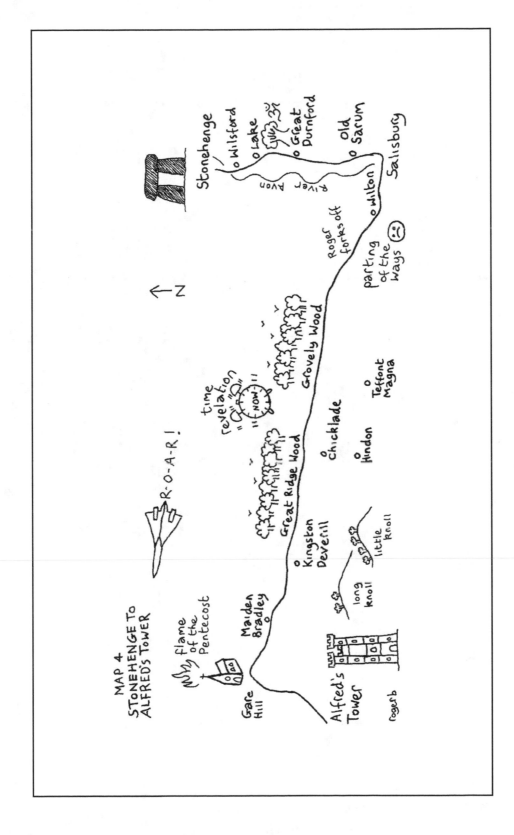

MAP 4
STONEHENGE TO
ALFRED'S TOWER

N ←

R-O-A-R!

Flame of the Pentecost

Gare Hill

Maiden Bradley

Alfred's Tower

roger b

long knoll

little knoll

Kingston Deverill

Great Ridge Wood

time revelation "NOW!!"

Grovely Wood

Chicklade

Hindon

Teffont Magna

Roger forks off

parting of the ways

Wilton

Salisbury

River Avon

Old Sarum

Great Durnford

Lake

Wilsford

Stonehenge

Woodhenge, Stonehenge and free-born Englishmen

Yesterday's twilit visit to Stonehenge evoked deep brooding thoughts far into the night. Still, Saturday's another day.

From the diary:

Cold all night. Sleep finally comes as birds awake and start their twittering chatter. Tea first this morning for the warmth that's in it. Broke camp and walked through the woods and up the road to the site of Woodhenge which we are excited to see. But we found ourselves let down. The location of timber posts now marked with dull short concrete pillars. No-one seems to know if this was a henge or a roundhouse or a hall or something else altogether. We larked about a bit and read the information board. Not a very inspiring place, all ancientness has seemingly left it, now it's just an enclosure of mundane speculation. A disappointment really. It's an oddly discomfiting day today, very cold but somehow edgy, close and airless at the same time.

We walk across country through fields to Stonehenge.

Unlike last night, there are hordes of tourists. We had a cup of tea then had to pay 10p to get into the big round stoniness. Can't help feeling that if you walk there it should be free.

Touch stone. Sat stone. Allowed. Walked stone. Thunk. Rested against stone. Thunk again and mused, feeling cold and not liking the crowd or the vibe.

We looked at each other and with a nod were gone, away from the stones and the visitors. More tea before we go yonder. Where to now? We don't know but it seems we need to strike out west towards Glastonbury, although no clear route presents itself.

We take the track we found last night towards the settlement of Lake via various seemingly disregarded barrows. Managed to get lost. Ended up in Wilsford. Along silent road. Silence. To Lake and quidsville. Then to a place called Wilsford cum Lake. Beautiful powerful chequerboard Lake House. Around here some other kind of Deep England, posh houses seemingly hidden from the hoi polloi - who would ever come to Wilsford cum Lake and know these places existed? It's a pass-me-by place where rich lives are lived out in secret.

We plunge back into the woods, our natural habitat, to camp near the top of the hill. I went for water. The man in the posh house said we couldn't camp here but we did anyway. He came by later with his armed gamekeeper as we were cooking dinner, came down into the woods, see what we're up to. He seemed quite angry and said again we couldn't camp here and had better move on. I gave him a free-born Englishman rap, explained we were on a pilgrimage, had been on the road for three weeks, just passing through, expected to be let to pass without incident or hostility, no-one up to now has stood in our way and if you please we will be gone come tomorrow and you wouldn't know we had ever been here. He seemed a little taken aback and then said he was glad to see we had stones around and containing the campfire. He actually seemed to ruminate on my free-born Englishman tirade and cooled out a bit. Said we could stay one night, be off in the morning.

Jeez it's not like the Ridgeway.

Dinner was guess what? Rice and lentils, potatoes and onions, cheese and bread. Never get sick of it. Always hungry. Was quite a nice little camp in the beech trees really, plenty of fallen wood for the fire, in the shelter of a bank. Sat around the fire writing letters and the diary and it started to gently rain. Roger and Madhead playing Jews' harps, boing-a-boing-a-boing, good stuff, donga dunga donga, dunga, hirschhhh, big blow out and whoooshy inhale. More good stuff. Goodnight. Oh yeah, saw a brown hare this afternoon, really close. We'd seen them before at a distance playing with cows, darting in and out of their legs while the cows went mad, trying to stomp them. And in these woods tonight a stag ran by, just a young one with little stumpy horns yet, or is that a doe? Oh I doe not know, and two bunnies, playing very close by, jumping and chasing, as we sat quiet. One thing we have learned. Animals play, animals have the same occasional delight in just being alive and happy mischief as we do.

2022

Madhead: As with my comments for Day 19, Stonehenge is now a bit of a disappointment. I'd forgotten that we'd also been disappointed fifty years ago. Even though the admission was only the price of half a pint of beer.

On the other hand, our camp that night, in those woods, was as magical as it could get. The landowner and his minder were a bit of a caution but all's well that ends well as they say. Happy bunnies everywhere. It was good to be back on the road.

Roger: The distant man with the gun finally caught up with us then, and Squash stood his ground on behalf of one and all. The 'owner' of the wood wasn't expecting to hear such an articulate tirade from a scruffy hippie rogue. I've always admired Squash's ability to speak well and speak out in the heat of such moments, did I say that earlier, I'll say it again. Anyway, we only wanted to borrow this man's wood for one night in the same way as he was borrowing it for a bit longer. Shame he didn't get to hear the Jews' harp concert, unless its mysterious twangs wafted over to his house in the night.

That idea of Squash having his grim Stonehenge face replaced with a hole in his life size photograph in the visitor centre is surreal beyond belief.

Squash: That visit came back to life in 2018 when English Heritage, in celebration of 100 years of public ownership of Stonehenge, mounted an exhibition of historic photographs taken by visitors. This is from their website:

In 1918, local barrister Cecil Chubb and his wife Mary gave Stonehenge to the nation. This public-spirited decision marked a turning point in the history of Stonehenge and its fortunes. Throughout 2018 we remembered and celebrated that gift, discovering what this iconic monument means to people today. We asked you to send us photos and stories that captured your time at Stonehenge.

The response to the appeal was incredible, with uploads of more than 1400 images dating as far back as the 1870s. There were so many amazing submissions we decided to create an exhibition. We wrote to everyone who had sent in their photographs and from the replies received we selected 144 we felt best represented Stonehenge's recent history.

In response to that appeal I sent in the photo Roger took of me looking cold and surly and it was selected to be part of the exhibition. Sometime later I was asked by English Heritage for permission to blow the photograph up and mount it on a board with the face cut out so that visitors could pop their heads through the hole for a souvenir pic, as a sort of end-of-the-pier type jollification. Why not, thought I, and suggested I could go down there and pop my own 70 year old face through my 23 year old head. They thought that was a fun idea and good publicity. It was all arranged until, sadly, the Covid outbreak put the kibosh on it. The exhibition ran to September 2022.

Strange dreams, Zen musings and more kindness from strangers

Sunny Sunday morning in the woods. It's very noticeable, but probably not surprising, how the weather has a distinct effect on the mood of our travellers.

Seeing all the very posh houses yesterday in Wilsford cum Lake and being on the outside of the tourists at Stonehenge got me wondering if we three really were magic travellers like hobbits and elves (as I thought we were) or if, in fact, in Tolkien's upper-middle-class England, the Shire, we would have been regarded as interloping and unwelcome orcs. When I think now of Bilbo and Frodo in their commodious Bag End house and the threat to Middle Earth that Tolkien painted I realise that I was probably part of that threat - the overrunning of romantically-imagined privilege-ridden Merrie Olde Englande by rat-faced working-class scum and incoming folk with darker skin. Fear of the upstart and the foreigner. We three seemed to be passing insularly through an England in which I suddenly feel I didn't quite belong. If I am not actually an orc, the best I could hope for would be to be a forelock-tugging gardener like that obedient and devoted servant Sam Gamgee. Tolkien later said that Sam was the real hero of the story, he really did.

Hmm, yes, we dispossessed peasants are always painted as heroes when we do the unquestioning bidding of our masters. It's the same with "The Wind in the Willows" and those complacent gay old bachelors, Badger, Ratty and Mole who seemingly never did any work, and that arrogant loathsome fucker Toad. I would definitely have been one of the weasels or stoats in that story, struggling to raise my kids against all the odds, poaching rabbits and squatting Toad Hall to escape our miserable damp hovels. God, how the ruling elite hated and feared the plebs – except when there's work to be done or people to be sacrificed in some war – then we were suddenly the salt of the fucking earth or indomitable lion-hearted Tommies. We were expected to devotedly follow them even unto death. Usually ours, not theirs. Hey ho. Anyway, that's enough of that Commie talk, away we go on another day in the very large outdoors.

From the dishevelled old diary this Sunday:

Sunny morning. Bizarre dreams last night, was in an amazing house like The Magic Theatre in Herman Hesse's "Steppenwolf", hundreds of doors, each one opening onto weird things, one a cliff, one a blazing kitchen, one with a half-built roof and loads of construction vehicles, one the fire brigade, one a glittering ballroom, one a glasshouse full of exotic plants – and all these people too from everywhere - all the Cosmic Capers Club folk, hundreds of others that I never think about, um Ruth and Pat and later, having survived the uncertain thrills of the various rooms, there was a reception, Tina looking transfigured beautiful in evening gown and Chris in dress suit. Me in rags. They say a house in your dreams represents your Self and the many rooms are different parts of your mind and soul and your possibilities and potentials. There were scary rooms and party rooms and many locked doors, some marked PRIVATE, and other rooms still under construction.

Madhead was up first for water and Roger was off meditating. Me reading a little of Roger's book "*Selling Water by the River*", a Zen tract which tells me that "*Zen*

maintains that there is absolutely nothing to attain and nothing to get. Why would you pay for water by the river? Who, when they hear there is nothing to be attained, would want to go there?" Breakfast is porridge and buckwheat and a bowl of tea.

We pack up and take the bridleway to Great Durnford, stopping to get more water and to say farewell and thank you to the gamekeeper's master, mostly to shameface him I think. We left the camp looking untouched as though no-one had been there, dousing the fire, chucking the fire-blackened rocks down the slope and scuffing leafmould over the wet ashes. No doubt he will go and have a look and all he'll see is the mystical number three that Roger chalked on a Beech trunk to give him something to ponder.

The track went on down down down beautiful secrecy path to a tiny footbridge over the River Avon which looks clear and deep enough for swimming but by now the weather has turned cloudy and cold. Called at the Black Horse Inn for tobacco, me going through a door which I shouldn't and nearly getting eaten by massive barking growling dogs, hahaha was like another door in the Magic Theatre. Leisurely walk then to Old Sarum, first along a virtually lost footpath which was marked on the map but was completely overgrown, then along a nice old track. Me getting water and sugar from a house further down. Kind man laid a pound of sugar on me, just like that. Nice one. Sat in the earthworks ditch and made a fire, drank tea and got cooking the dinner. Rice, lentils, vegetables, hiziki, miso, cheese. Roger seems to have a limitless supply of hiziki seaweed and dark miso paste which is strong and salty.

While cooking along come two Salisbury school freaks, Nick, a Hawkwind and Pink Fairies fan and Steve who is very quiet. Nick laying some bread on us which was really kind. Far out. We seem to have become some sort of sadhus, poor holy men to whom people feel compelled to give alms for the good of their own souls. Ate dinner and afterwards made a good big pot of tea in the billy-can which we all shared. Nice. Rapped a little, mostly easy silence. When they split Steve gave us bread too for our quest. Thank you Nick and Steve, quite amazing, schoolboys giving us money. After they left we wandered around a bit, seeing the old cathedral foundations.

Old Sarum is a nice spot. We could see the "new" cathedral spire, far off down in the valley in Salisbury, couldn't figure out why they would want to move it but supposed it was to do with the workings of money and power. Bumped into some more freaks who were poking around and went with them back to where our campfire had been, got it blazing again, smoked loads of their dope and drank tea and laughed felt very silly, stoned again in fact. They went and we crashed out in the open by the fire. Sleeping in the moat at Old Sarum. Far out. Wood fire rustling, trees swaying gently across the stars above, ghostly Barn Owl goes silently over.

2022

Madhead: Old Sarum is another magical place but with a lot less of the touristy stuff. A place to sit and wonder at and imagine being there in the olden days (I mean more than fifty years ago of course). Woodhenge, in its glory, would have been a wonder to behold too.

Like I said earlier, the kindness of strangers ... Those schoolboys must have had a Saturday job, or a lot of pocket money, to be able to afford to give money away to a bunch of weirdos disguised as pilgrims. I wonder where they are now. I'd like to pay them back. I could also sing them a song or play a nice tune or two on my tambourine as a form of compound interest.

Roger: I recall there was a sense of purpose underlying our happy go lucky vision quest, cutting ties, looking for what next, or just finding somewhere more interesting than Reading to live in!

When we got to the sanctuary of Old Sarum some kind of penny dropped, suddenly Glastonbury felt like the wrong place for me to be going, and an urge to head off on my own arose. Like, hey, I'm off now. I remember silently wrestling with this painful decision to break away from our fellowship but very few details are available in my cerebral archive.

Squash: Old Sarum was peace itself after everyone else had gone. It was finally warm enough to sleep outside without a tent, just sky above. My favourite thing.

A day of changing fortunes

Diary entry this Monday:

Woke up after a warm night and dry in the big Old Sarum ditch. Cold oats and buckwheat and raisins for breakfast. Nice. Great view of Salisbury Cathedral whither we are bound. Walked into Salisbury about 9 o'clock, nice sunshine-groovy. Stopped in a fifties style café for tea. Town centre. People. Cars. Lots of both. And buses. Had a wash and brush-up in the public bogs, washed our hair too. Nice. Scored some food from rip-off respectable health-food store. Spent quids. Into the Cadena Café for a cup of tea. Madhead's back-strap split as we were coming out and he bodged it up with some nylon cord.

Went down to the pleasant grassy Choristers Green outside the Cathedral and admired the homely Cathedral Close, nice setting and row of attractive houses, where Ted Heath lives and blows tunes on the sexy saxophone, allegedly. Went in the Cathedral which is an impossibly beautiful building, the architecture is incredible, the power of the church made visible in geometry and physics when most lived in wattle, daub and thatch. But the grandeur, the Power and the Glory made me uneasy. If I were a Christian, a dissenter I would be.

The business bullshit whole Christian hypocrisy started to come down heavy on me so I sidled off and waited for Madhead and Roger outside. I was particularly affected by a stained glass window with paratroopers in it and I thought this is all wrong. While I understand the need to remember with respect those souls who have been killed by war I couldn't square pictures of men in uniform clutching guns with a religion supposedly built on the message of peace and love that Jesus taught. Maybe I'm just naïve, I dunno. Gathered again outside we bumped into one of the freaks from last night's shenanigans who rolled some up and got us all stoned again. Ate bread and Yeastrel (a savoury spread which helped Britain win the war) and peanut butter and then got tea from the tea machine in the cathedral cloisters to unclag our gummy mouths.

After lummoxing around for a while we split Salisbury that afternoon on the Wilton Road via Quidhampton village. Roger suddenly dropped a bombshell by announcing that he's not into this walk anymore, a coupla days since, so we hopelessly helplessly sat a bit and he said he'll keep with us a day or two anyway. He wants to not spend all his bread so he can get some carpentry together. Seems like we're at some sort of turning point, hanging in limbo. This is a shock to me and I'm hoping it's just a glitch and he'll change his mind.

Nearly in Wilton we were accosted by a strange blue-eyed bum with just a battered old briefcase. Odd, he acted like he knew us, like we were his old mates. Maybe it's the Brotherhood of the Wanderer. He said he was going down Devon way and asked for money which we gave him. Through Wilton, pausing for an ice-cream on the grass of St Mary & St Nicholas, the most incredible classical church looking like a Roman temple, part of the grand Wilton Estate. We took the hot uphill track to Grovely Wood which is massive and ancient and will take us a long way west into Somerset. There is a very long "Roman Road" through it from south-east to north- west, probably a ley line. Went to consult the Ordnance Survey map, our indispensable guide to finding footpaths and wooded places for camp and fire. No map. Where's map? Map gone. Lost it. Went back a mile or so but couldn't find it. Distress. This was a weird feeling, feel suddenly undone and unhinged, like when you find yourself in a foreign country and you don't know any of the language or recognise any of the food. Lost map lost me.

Went on into the woods, trusting to memory and luck. My head all at odds with itself. Made a fire. Burnt the rice. Dinner was burnt rice, lentils, potatoes and onions, Yeastrel and tea. Roger's pretty Indian cloth caught fire. Later a third of an orange each. Wrote letters to Wizz and Dibsy begging for money (but had no address for them to send it to - as if they would anyway). Just a way of sending a message to the universe, help we are broke. Shared a stick of rhubarb dipped in sugar.

This is a nice wood, I like it. There are noises in the dark. We heard lots of movement, night-time squeals and rustlings in the undergrowth. Suddenly close-by there's a loud barking cough in the dark which we hope is a deer. Madhead and Roger seem a bit freaked out by the living noises and scuttle into the tent but I prefer to sleep outside. I have a nice stash of firewood next to me and fall asleep to the clicks and murmurs of a dying fire and the cool night air whispering in my face.

Madhead: Roger's bombshell really was a shattering thing. The shrapnel was hanging in mid-air, ready to fall in slow motion over the next coupla days into my heart. Things were about to become never the same again.

Grovely Wood was good though. The track through was probably only a loggers' ride but it gave a good perspective and certainly felt like a leyline. That tunnel effect.

And noises at night still give me the willies – especially foxes – it's the suddenness. It's a wonder I still have my skin.

Roger: Adding these little addenda and still being a curious wayward creature half a century later, and with very little clear recollection of detail to go on, the urge to dream and ramble doth arise at every turn.

So, to be brief, I refer to all my experiences of stepping into all the cathedrals I have been in, in one go. Magnificent architectural poem of contemplation, hundreds of years in the building. Yet, it is the space it encloses that takes the breath away and quickens the heart. The usefulness of emptiness as the *Tao Te Ching* says.

Then I'm thinking of tiny humble chapels or little wayside shrines, or ragged prayer flags on mountainsides.

Squash: That weird lonesome travelling bum turned up like a Tarot card. It has been pointed out to me that he showed up on Day 22 and that 22 in the Tarot is the number of The Fool, usually portrayed as a beggar or vagabond. In many esoteric systems of Tarot card interpretation the Fool is interpreted as the protagonist of a story and the Major Arcana is the path the Fool takes through the great mysteries of life. The Fool depicts a youth walking joyfully into the world. He is taking his first steps, and he is exuberant, joyful, excited. He carries nothing with him except a small sack, caring nothing for the possible dangers that lie in his path.

We see this day the trouble with getting stoned. I get forgetful and lose my bearings. There was a strange accumulation of events that day that started so promising. The town, the people rushing past, the thorough wash, the cathedral, the freaks, Roger's bombshell, the travelling bum, losing the map, burning the rice and Roger's cloth, the noises abroad in the dark, a feeling of unease.

But then, the dossbag, the murmuring fire, the drifting woodland breath, and peace and sleep. The feeling that everything will be alright.

The day as foretold is come

On the day we set out on this venture, Roger consulted the *I Ching* which gave us hexagram 60 Limitation - "*the thrift that sets fixed limits upon expenditure. In the moral sphere it means the fixed limits that the superior man sets upon his actions – the limits of loyalty and disinterestedness*".

The moving lines in the hexagram in turn gave us a second hexagram 41 Decrease – "*Decrease combined with sincerity brings about supreme good fortune, without blame*" and "*if a time of scanty resources brings out an inner truth, one must not be ashamed of simplicity*". More ominously it also said "*when three persons journey together, their number decreases by one*".

☐ Six in the third place means:
When three people journey together,
Their number decreases by one.
When one man journeys alone,
He finds a companion.

From the diary on this Tuesday:

I woke up during the night for a while, stoked up the dying fire into a good blaze, enjoying the fiery sparkles fleeting skywards in a funnel of smoke. I love the warmth and light of the fire on the dossbag and the cool night woodland air wafting over my face. Had a great sleep. Breakfast was a cold feast of oats, buckwheat, nuts and raisins. We seem to have reinvented muesli I guess.

After our breakfast Roger says he has decided to definitely split. My stomach and spirits sink. It's not done to question your mate, knowing he has been soul-searching to come to this decision so we ask nothing. Gotta be a man about it, even if your heart is breaking.

I say well I am going on anyway, even if I have to go on my own. I would've too, but I have this strange conundrum. I am a part-time loner who doesn't really like being alone. Actually I do like being alone sometimes, but being alone all the time doesn't feel right. Hard to explain, but I feel more self-conscious when on my own, watching my own doings. I'm hoping to hell that Madhead will carry on with the journey, with me. When we left Reading he and I sort of decided that, whatever happened, we were not coming back, thought we might settle in Frome even though we knew nothing about the place. It was just a little town on the map that spoke to us. Pregnant pause and Madhead nods affirmative. Thank fuck for that. We share out the essentials. He and Roger exchange packs, Madhead needs the bigger backpack to carry the rest of the tent. So grateful that he is continuing and that he doesn't mind loading his pack more.

Walked back out onto the old Roman Road through Grovely Wood where we took our sad and sweet farewells, he going one way, us the other. Roger is mooching back to Salisbury then hitch-hiking to Bath to see some people, to other dreams and other realities …. Goodbye Roger I shall miss you (as I am now) and your madness and good songs and Leonine strength … see you soon old friend.

Madhead and I plunging deeper into woods, mile after mile of straight Roman Road, great weight on our backs, hot thundery sunshine. Stopping at Grovely Lodge, and later in the sun for lunch of wholemeal bread and marg and Yeastrel and peanut butter. Split the customary orange, sharing desolating halves, not thirds this time. Presently we come to the end of the woods and, having no map and being lost, we turn south towards Dinton. The sign says two miles but it seemed twice as far as that. Country miles. Scored a Hovis loaf and tobacco and oranges at the village shop and walked out, very hot and weary, on the quiet road towards Hindon. Found a wood by the side of the road to camp in. This was not our customary beech wood, but was predominantly oak. It has a different character altogether. There isn't the dry clear ground beneath the trees, it's all damp vegetation, soggy soil and giant wood ants.

I went back a way to a cottage to get water. Kindly motherly lady sat me down in her homely cluttered lounge and got all her maps out to show me the way and gave me yesterday's newspaper to read. Looking at her maps I see that we are veering way too far north so I need to remember to steer southwards tomorrow. Back at the camp I read the paper a while, news from a distant star, and put the dinner on. The fallen firewood was much decayed and wet and rotten and needed sustained encouragement and blowing to burn. These woods full of flies. Dinner was rice and lentils, onions, carrots, hiziki and miso, our friend leaving us his magic supplies. Our first dinner without Roger, a big strange empty Roger-shaped hole in our insularity. Stewed the rhubarb afterwards with some sugar. It was divine. Getting gnat-bitten all over, got into the tent to escape the flies. Wrote a long letter to my mum, both Madhead and me feeling a bit sad.

2022

Madhead: When soothsaying becomes reality, it's still kind of unbelievable. A bit like ignoring the giant asteroid of climate change or something.

Roger left a bigger hole than he actually occupied when he filled it. Since our paths forked, for the life of me I can't remember ever seeing him in the flesh again, although I'm told that he popped up in Glastonbury soon after we arrived. Memories eh? The thing is, no matter how much you think of someone and remember all the good times, it's so nice to just share the same space for a while, look into each other's eyes and breathe.

Interesting thing about Squash and me both wanting to live in Frome. Why Frome? And how on earth did I eventually get to live there 10 years later and then stay for 35 years? It's a wonderful place, that's why.

Still, chin up lads, there's miles yet to cover. Mapless.

Roger: It's difficult to read the responses of Squash in his journal, and Martin in his recollection, to my sudden decision to forsake their company. It's quite a thing to look back and realize you hurt someone a long time ago... even if it's a long time ago. As I write it feels like right now and I feel sad about that parting. I must have had a jumble of thoughts swarming in my nineteen-year-old hippie head. If only I could reach for my own journal and read what was going on for me.

There was something about those three weeks in the company of my good friends, walking ancient trails, landscape and woodland, living outdoors, walking with home on back. Something very strong and powerful and real. Running on my own juices, doing my Zen sitting, getting back to nature, seeking my own vision of how to live. I wanted to carry on like that.

And I was really enjoying the break from a somewhat dope-fuelled life. Getting stoned with those folk we met in Old Sarum, I think I felt plunged right back in to what I didn't want and got into a depressive funk. I just remember a feeling of dread rising in me about heading for Glastonbury. Glastonbury had already become a sort of bustling hippie dream epicentre which unsettled me more than I wanted to admit at the time maybe. Anyhow must have been a strong feeling that I decided to make my own way and let my friends down.

Through the mists of time I offer my sincere apologies for becoming a Roger-shaped absence!

Grovely Woods may not have helped either! I found it creepy as soon as we entered. Interesting what you found out about it. The gruff loud barking echoing round the trees was surely the rutting call of a deer but I did not know that at the time, and was imagining some crazy giant off the leash mastiff on the prowl, maybe it was my own black dog coming to hassle me... so not exactly a peaceful night's sleep.

Squash: Grovely Wood is famously "haunted" by the ghosts of the four Danish Handsel sisters who were blamed by the local peasantry for an outbreak of small-pox in 1737 and were murdered as witches and buried beneath beech trees in the wood. Three of the four trees survive and have become places of honour and remembrance by modern witches. Also said to be haunted by the Burcombe Woodsman who was hanged for poaching on the Wilton Estate. The latter an-nounces his presence with the snapping of twigs and a throaty cough, just as we heard last night. Years later Roger told me that he was freaked out and spooked by Grovely Wood. Makes you wonder.

Roger's message to us when first asked to write his recollections:

Dear the two of you,

I felt a few pangs as I tried to write about that day.
All of it, and everything, including losing touch over the years, what you say is true Martin.
Sorry I forked off.
Those three weeks leading up to that were magical. Amazing to attempt to recall them.

Squash, the headstone idea made me laugh, I'll think about that.
And yes that would be great to carry on with the comments. I could use the pseud-onym Rogershapedspace.

Squash: When Roger sent me this message I reminded him of his longstanding habit of suddenly declaring "I'm off now" so I suggested for his headstone the epitaph "Sorry I forked off". Hahaha. Love him.

For anyone wondering, Roger will continue to offer his observations on the Walk as Roger shaped space.

Trio decreased by one, a new day dawns and the nature of time reveals itself

After yesterday's sad parting with Roger we wake to a different sort of day and, eventually, settle into a new smoother groove as we adjust.

Diary notes on this Wednesday's westward movements:

Slept in the tent last night – always seems colder in there than kipping outside, but the flies drove us in. Made breakfast muesli which we ate in bed. Can't be arsed trying to get the rotten oak to burn. Away early and along this sunny road to Teffont Magna, an unusually strange looking place sheltering under the wooded ridge but a nice village with nice people. Beautiful sunshine, clean air and a light refreshing breeze. We are basically a bit lost without a map but it doesn't seem to matter too much. Up a track towards the woods – o woe the last house is empty. We were relying on it for water. Crossed the roaring madness of the A303 road - yuk - made me momentarily want to stick out my thumb. But off we go down a muddy track and get properly lost in the peace of the woods.

Stopped a long stop midday. When you are out in the open all day at this time of year the daylight hours are seemingly endless. Laid around soaking up sunbeams for two hours, watching the doings and toings and froings of a little metallic green bug. Had an amazing picnic, half a small Hovis each with peanut butter and Yeastrel and half an orange and the last of the water. Madhead fell asleep and I resumed watching the bug. For hours I watched him and, as far as I could see, he didn't do a lot, apart from moving all the time. Sometimes he would climb to the top of a blade of grass, fall off and continue his perambulations. Sometimes he went under a dried fragment of a leaf and then reappeared and resumed walking. Sometimes he doubled back on himself. It was all very puzzling, loads of activity to no discernible purpose. Maybe he was eating things too small for me to see. Maybe he was put off by my looming over him, watching his every move. Made me think how like humans he was. Lots of action, little apparent purpose.

Then, while I ruminated, I had a sudden, overwhelming, quite mind-shattering insight into the nature of time. All the chains that keep us ploughing our furrow through time fell away and I realised TIME as a dark, not unfriendly, ocean that sort of extended in all directions and that there was an endless amount of it. YOU COULD NEVER NOT HAVE ENOUGH TIME. You could help yourself to as much as you wanted, it was all around you, you could dip a ladle in it and there was always more, it was endless, a magic porridge pot of Time. There was no past and no future. Everything that ever happened or could ever happen could only ever happen NOW. There was nothing else. NOTHING ELSE EXISTS. The meaning of Time was exactly the same as the meaning of being alive. Time is literally ever-present. Time never stops or disappears. Time doesn't move on, we do. Time is merely how we measure change, change that always happens in the present. Time is an illusion in which we swim. These are hopeless words but I actually experienced it, deep and dark and whistling in the nowhere. This was not an intellectual revelation, it was a body and soul immersion, like coming adrift in a massive void, and it was not in the least unpleasant. Phew. It was this walk and that bug wot dunnit to me.

Later I woke Madhead up because I didn't want him to dry up in the sun and feel terrible. We needed to get on and find some water. Got lost in the woods seeking an assumed Great West Route and all we found was the A Three 0 fucking Three again, a great west route sure enough but not what we wanted. Had to walk along it for a way, hot, weary, dusty, lorries whamming by and roadworks and traffic jams on Woodbine Hill. A house a mile down the road proved empty too. Strange karma. No water yet, only a little left in the small bottle. We wearied on another half a mile. No answer at the next house but at least have made it to the edge of the map that follows the one I lost. Feels good to be able to get our bearings again. Now just sitting outside the house getting it together to walk on to Chicklade when a Dormobile pulled up and two smiling sunshine happy kids got out and walked towards the front door. We asked them for water, they went in and it turned out their mother had been in all the time. Probably frightened the life out of her, two weirdos at the threshold. Anyway, gladdened now, thank God for lovely children and for water.

Up the track towards the high trees, the Great Ridge Wood. Steep and tiring going but we eventually find a nice grassy space though still a lot of flies about. I guess we're intruding on them, not them on us. Put the tent up, collected wood and got a cup of tea together on a small fire. Ah! the power of teabags. Refreshed we crawl into our fly-proof stuffy tent for rest and fags.

Later cook up dinner of rice and lentils, carrots and potatoes, miso. Madhead and I lying by the fire rapping, later our first attempt at baking with Scofa flour in the billy can. Madhead mixed the dough and we plonked it in the fire. Alas the fire must've still been too hot. The bread rose beautifully but the outside was burnt black and the inside was gluey. However we salvaged that for later use. Made another bowl of tea and rapped some more about the Time revelation, how it was a trick and there was all the time in the ever-present now to do things properly, coolly and graciously. Into bed and so to sleep.

2022

Madhead: Pretty Zen stuff about time and the now. We could talk about it for hours and still only be at the beginning. The Australian First Nations people, I believe, see time as a lake and that one can pitch up in at any point.

It's funny how the memory plays tricks but one thing I remember about the Scofa flour is that I have never, ever, used it again.

Roger shaped space: Squash has invited me to continue my presence as the Roger shaped space.

I forked off, where did I go with my stubble head? I think I went to Bath to drop in on Russ where I probably had a Bath, then I headed for a brief almost penniless sojourn in the far north, maybe to complete my own journey with a different destination. I remember sitting at a table in my scruff clothes rapping with two Japanese backpacker girls in the kitchen room of a youth hostel in Inverness. "We thought you were Japanese when we saw you. You make very good Zen monk!" Hey.

Meanwhile on the Glastonbury trail, Squash meets a Zen master in the form of a metallic green bug and has an extraordinary experience of realization.

As my stubble-head turned into brush-head. I did buy some carpentry tools, enrolled in an evening class, made a simple and beautiful box, and discovered I could make things with my hands.

Squash: That realisation about the nature of time was quite shattering, but in a useful mind-altering way. You know when you have a déjà vu experience, it sometimes lasts for longer than usual and you can feel and chase the ripples of it? Well this experience of time being all around you in all directions and always there and infinitely renewable hung on for long minutes while my mind gasped and gaped at the enormity of it. I could actually see it – a huge black infinite ocean – and could feel it and the reassurance that came with it, that everything was alright, no need to panic about anything, there is no pressure. I can almost recapture the feeling to this day, can taste it, but can't quite immerse myself in it as happened that day all those years ago.

Contemplating now Roger's departure is weird. Although he was four years younger than us he was somehow older than us too and the dynamic we shared was heavily influenced by his spirituality and his quest. It lent a noble stringency to our doings and kept us high-minded. I didn't see it at the time, we just missed him, but I think now that Madhead and I became more childish after he left. Or should I say child-like? We reverted from men to boys, I think, while Roger was having a stab at being a man and made himself a box. A simple and beautiful box of course.

Hahaha. Life is so funny.

A Taste of Paradise and a longing for the company of a woman

Thursday diary notes:

Last night was the first really warm night in the tent. We had breakfast in bed again, delicious muesli. We live and lounge like lords of old.

Being back within the frame of the following Ordnance Survey sheet after losing the preceding one means we are again able to put names to places. We are camped in the Great Ridge Wood, high above the surrounding countryside. It's better up here, away from the roads and the bounded suburbs and villages. Plenty of sky for a roof and picture windows on all sides between the trees for the views and for the wind to frolic in.

We left the tent and all our stuff and got ourselves together to walk through the woods and down the track to Chicklade for shopping. No shops in Chicklade so we trucked on in pleasant clear sunshine up and over the hill to Hindon. It's so nice, walking without a backpack, unburdened, feel about 10 years old, breezing along with my friend in the sunshine. Hindon is a very pretty place with a good vibe, a place that seems comfortable with itself. We drank a pint of gold top milk and shared a Bounty bar. "Bounty - The Taste of Paradise" went the adverts and they were right. Can't believe how wonderful chocolate is, so thrilled with its divine taste we laughed aloud with every bite - any minute expecting a bikini-clad goddess from the adverts to emerge from the shop. Absolutely mind-blowing after our austere diet and monastic lives.

I think we have used up our bodies' reserves over the last 25 days and so anything we eat tastes fabulous. I was never too fussed about food, always skinny and rarely hungry, but now I would eat anything that was careless enough to come near my mouth. Scored our groceries and got a bit of cheese cheap too. Onions an incredible 18p a pound so we left them. Trucked back in growing heat, got our water from a nice lady who was just about to enjoy fruit squash at a table on the front lawn with her friend. How dignified that seemed. Struggled back up the track, blazing hot, and arrived nearly exhausted at Saffron Cottage. Changed into shorts and sandals, packed our lunch in Madhead's shoulder bag, and padded through the woods like two Mahatma Ghandis going for a cleansing dip. Found a pleasant grassy space, lunched and sun-bathed until we could stand it no more.

Back at camp Madhead was having quite a scene with loads of little insects running up and down his legs and in his dossbag. Probably crabs. We crashed out through the heat of the afternoon and woke up at 6.30 with thick heads. Muggily collected wood and got the dinner together. We had rice, potatoes, cheese and the inside of our burnt Scofa loaf. Followed by tea and chocolate. Delicious. Then to my diary. Wrote letters late to the girls and boys of the Cosmic Capers Club. Saw a handsome fox lurking about, that sly bold Reynardine. What's he up to?

Sings that wonderful Fairport Convention song, the one that Sandy Denny sings and makes the hairs on your neck, and other things, stand up:

One evening as I rambled
Among the leaves so green
I overheard a young woman
Converse with Reynardine
Her hair was black, her eyes
Were blue, her lips as red as wine
And he smiled to gaze upon her
Did that sly, bold Reynardine
She said, "Kind sir, be civil
My company forsake
For in my own opinion
I fear you are some rake"
"Oh no" he said, "no rake am I
Brought up in Venus' train
But I'm seeking for concealment
All along the lonesome plain"
"Your beauty so enticed me
I could not pass it by
So it's with my gun I'll guard you
All on the mountain side"

"And if by chance you should look
For me, perhaps you'll not me find
For I'll be in my castle
Inquire for Reynardine"
Sun and dark she followed him
His teeth did brightly shine
And he led her up a-the mountains
*Did that sly, bold Reynardine ** *

* "Reynardine" from the 1969 album *Liege & Lief* by Fairport Convention

Had another bowl of tea and went to bed. Wished I had a woman. I think that chocolate has given me the horn, overcoming the starvation of my libido. Couldn't sleep for hours, that's the trouble with snoozing the afternoon through.

2022

Madhead: I don't think that, at my age, I could walk very far with a rucksack full of house and homeware like we did fifty years ago. To go untrammelled into the yonder nowadays, I carry a Swiss Army knife, Ventolin and handkerchief in my trouser pockets. Oh, and a knapsack with a bottle of water, maybe a snack, map(s), camera, sunglasses, fleece, waterproofs, wallet, car keys, phone, binoculars, compass and whistle. And, if hilly or there will be lots of stiles to clamber over, one of my walking sticks. "Travel light" is the rule.

I think the "crabs" were actually sheep ticks. Nasty little buggers climb to the top of vegetation and come aboard as you brush past. Not wearing shorts is a good defence.

Roger shaped space: In order to fully experience the ecstatic visions of the southern sea goddess participants would undergo weeks of austerity before ingestion of the chocolate and coconut preparation, usually in the form of 'bars'.

When chocolate first appeared, and in its purest form, was it not 'taken' for its ecstatic and aphrodisiac qualities? A recreational drug for the gentry.

And these days you can do shamanic vision-seeking cacao ceremonies.

Archaic techniques of ecstasy in modern times. Click to enrol.

We set off with a purpose that we could not define, didn't want to, our path unrolling before us. Seeking the thing we could not grasp; we knew it when it was there and carried on when it wasn't.

Having wandered off on my own, for a short while finding it bleakfaced, solitary on mountainside, before returning to the throng.

Kerouac: *"I see a vision of a great rucksack revolution thousands or even millions of young Americans wandering around with rucksacks, going up to mountains to pray, making children laugh and old men glad, making young girls happy and old girls happier, all of 'em Zen Lunatics who go about writing poems that happen to appear in their heads for no reason and also by being kind and also by strange unexpected acts keep giving visions of eternal freedom to everybody and to all living creatures ..."*

Is that naïve and beautiful feeling of walking your walk without clutter still available to all? I hope so.

Squash: Whoever came up with the advert for Bounty Bars was a genius, often copied but never equalled. The coupling of sweet sweet chocolate and scantily-clad maidens was a winning combination to spark the longings of us ascetic wanderers bereft of the loving touch of either. Haha, as ongoing starvation of treats begins to take hold so do the fantasies of both increase.

And there's Roger enduring solitude on a mountainside.

The day of the three Cs

You never know what sights you will see on the trail, what human activity and what kindness you might meet. Sometimes you see things you wish you hadn't and sometimes you see things that are sublime and give you pause for thought and sometimes you see things that make you go aaargh gaaargh.

The diary for this Friday says this:

Sleep was a long time coming last night and when it did it burst into many complicated dreams. I dreamt that Roger and Madhead and I went to my childhood home, the very place in Emmer Green from whence we set out on this walk. I had a door key and it worked. The house had all the same ornaments and furniture from when I was a kid, but it turned out there was a severe woman living there (not my mum ... or was it?) who lived alone. Early forties she was ... Anyway we had to leave as I realised I didn't belong there anymore ...

Dreamt later that I was with my ex-girlfriend Sheila again, or for the first time again, and she was in love with me and me with her. Her parents were cool but very strict. Then they caught me smoking and went mad, Sheila ran off crying and, I knew this was going to happen, fell over and was either unconscious or dead. The dream ended with me walking away carrying her limp body in my arms and with tears rolling down my face ...

Talk about your brain buttoning up the past and leaving it behind. My two last homes swapped for walls of trees and a roof of leaves.

Breakfast muesli in our little all-purpose bowls, in the tent. Packed up which took ages, very heavy packs they seemed after a day not wearing them, and wound our way back through the woods, past where we saw the fox and away up Cratt Hill. Got to a junction of tracks, got a little diverted but found the right course again. Stopped by the woods towards Rook Hill and lunched on Hovis and lettuce and fish paste (yes we are that skint) and Yeastrel and half an orange each.

Resumed our way up the track where we suddenly startled a love-making couple who panicked and leapt apart at our appearance from around a grassy bank. I saw right into her ginger muff. Yer man's thing was bobbing for apples. Not far away was a fresh human turd. I don't know what part, if any, that played in the proceedings. The things you see! A gag-whiff and another whiff of an office romance there, keeping the life-force flowing uphill. We sniggered a bit and crossed the car-park where his travelling salesman's car was parked.

Then gradually becoming aware of a distant roaring noise that grew and grew until it crushingly pressed down from the heavens from horizon to horizon, the birds gone silent, lambs scattering in all directions. What the fuck weirdness was this? Then we saw it! A perfectly shaped white dart crossing the sky with a noise like the tantrums of the gods. Concorde. Wow! Never seen it before. What a beauty! What a deafening diabolical row! Felt the strangeness of the most ancient of places beneath our feet and the most modern of devilish devices in the air. Eventually it passed out of sight, trailing its monstrous coils of boiling thunder.

At the top of the track we exchanged good mornings with an old couple picnicking at a little table by their car. We crossed the road but they called us back and gave us coffee and three biscuits each. They were amazing people, from Formby, Lancs. He had retired from the police force at age 52 in 1957. Ever since they have been touring around all over the place, making their way now to a week's hotel holiday at Eastbourne. We talked about Lloret, Benidorm and San Sebastian, them telling us about a Spanish-speaking English cat from Birmingham who they wined and dined and who was ripping them off for their change the whole time. But they laughed about it – old guy said he enjoyed his company anyway and thought it was worth it. Cheery goodbyes, sincerely meant. You meet some of the nicest people on the road, and receive random acts of kindness that had become a pattern towards us of curiosity and blessings from strangers.

Down the track to Monkton Deverill – very hot and close by now as we amble through. Along the quiet road to Kingston Deverill where we stopped at the Post Office Stores and scoffed two ice-creams each and shared a Milky Way, our chocolate transport to the stars. I don't know what's wrong with us – we are craving sugar all the time. Got some water from an old dear with three dogs and sweated our way up Court Hill and stopped at the tumulus near the straggly wood which is a tall raucous rookery. Got dinner together – rice, lentils, potatoes, carrots, miso, cheese. Too hot to eat round the fire so we sat atop the tump and dug the stupendous view back over the land from whence we had come. The country around here is exceptionally beautiful, all rounded humps of hills and deep valleys in which nestle quiet villages. As we sat there ruminating Madhead said "well, cunt, coffee and Concorde, I think we've cracked it!" What did he mean?

Had nice tea after. We were now getting closer to magical Avalon. It's weird, there seems to be some force that makes each step seem harder to take. It's very subtle but there's some reluctance in it, we are sort of hedging around it, we have days to divert ourselves before arriving in Glastonbury for the Summer Solstice. I hope it doesn't rain tonight. Clouds are building up and we haven't bothered to pitch the tent. We had some more tea and retired to bed after dark. The rooks wouldn't settle until we did, cawing and cackling on. Us, not them. Built up the fire and rapped a bit more about this and that.

2022

Madhead: Now that was a day to remember! It's seared into my brain. You never forget the first time you meet a retired copper ... and I should have added "crap" into my alliterative observation.

I suppose the beginnings of that foot-dragging feeling was a kind of not wanting the whole trip to end. I could have sauntered for ever but, by now, we were very low on funds so there was also a tiny urge to go and earn a bit of cash somehow.

Roger shaped space: Holy wanderers receiving kindness and blessings from strangers, like Kerouac's vision.

Something about this thing.
What is that old time religion that's good enough for me?
Runs in the warp and the weft.

Squash: That was indeed a day to remember but, weirdly, I distinctly remembered Roger being there and laughing along with us as the chap jumped up leaving his amour spread-eagled and unfulfilled. I was so convinced of this that I had to question the Diary but, as per usual, the Diary was right, it was there after all and didn't age a day or lose its power of recall afterwards, unlike me. I find that odd and it was not the only time my memory proved unreliable, only to be corrected when I re-read the Diary for the first time after four decades. I must've carried Roger with me in spirit.

There have been many lamentations about the demise of Concorde but I'm glad its time has passed. Although I admired the brilliance of the technology and the sublime beauty of its form, this was a typically British White Elephant, designed to enable a gilded elite of 100 or so people to zoom across the Atlantic faster than a speeding bullet, while the Americans recognised the dawning of the age of mass air-transit and came up with the Boeing 747 which carried 500 passengers. They had Jumbo and we had Dumbo. The noise it made really was so horrendous that it was only allowed to fly flat out over the oceans. Thousands on the ground had to endure its deafening roar just for the benefit of a few rich people's self-importance.

I did like the rooks though. Always enjoy their busy chaotic racket which was altogether more bearable. I felt like they were talking about us and admiring our clothes and hairstyles.

Beautiful scenery, beautiful villages and the onset of hay fever

The diary, he say it's Saturday today and:

Didn't sleep until very late into the night again. At least it didn't rain and the sun came up clear and warm over the tump when we woke up at 7.30 with the rooks making their usual racket, cawing and clattering in the treetops. Breakfasted on a big bowl of muesli. Packed up and set off along the ridge of Rodmead Hill and down a track to Rodmead Farm.

Long Knoll and Little Knoll looking absolutely spectacular in the morning light, humpbacks breaching in an ocean of green. In fact all the countryside is beautiful round here. Madhead and I had an argument about something and nothing which flared up but was soon over. First squabble we've ever had. Up the track from the farm a flat-hatted racing man stopped in his swish motor and offered us a lift to Wincanton which was pretty groovy, but we dug to keep walking and we didn't want to go to Wincanton anyway. It's funny how cars are like forgotten things to us, not part of our world.

Arrived at Maiden Bradley, old settled pretty village. Scored two loaves, small, sort of nutty brown bread – 9 pence each! Apparently bread went up last Monday. Got more milk powder too and shared a Mars Bar. Never before realised that a Mars Bar is a feast of massive proportions and could actually blow your head off, all the way to Mars I guess. Went to the Somerset Arms pub which is across the road and is in Wiltshire anyway. Friendly people in there. Had two halves of bitter shandy each which, incredibly, made us feel half-pissed. Stopped to chat a little up the road with an old man and a young hairy guy tidying the garden of a cottage. Turned off in high spirits up the road towards Gaer or Gare Hill.

We take a track into the woods, smothering in the beautiful sight and scent of rhododendrons and honeysuckle and pine trees. Track goes down down down, finally crossing a tiny stream, then up and up very steep and hot, finally summiting near the quite modern-looking church that sits atop this landmark hill. We go over there. It turns out not to be modern, but Victorian, perfectly nipple-situated on the crest of windy Gare Hill overlooking the wide and flat, densely populated vale in which nestle Frome, Westbury, Radstock, Midsomer Norton, Trowbridge and, further away, Bradford-on-Avon and Bath. I wonder if Roger is there still.

The little church as expected is dedicated to St Michael and All Angels like all these hilltop ones on ley-lines. It is a beautifully ragged and beat building with a harmonium and, like all the churches around here, unlocked. We entered the modest mouldy-musty interior and I had a read of the damp Bible – the bit about the feeding of the multitudes, the loaves and fishes, a good magic trick that we could do with, never go hungry again. Then the bit about whosoever shall save his life will lose it, and whosoever will lose his life for Me shall save it. This resonates with the idea of ego-death achieved through transcendence or, in our case, repeated doses of LSD. I still don't like churches but this one's better than most, more humble, less grand.

Went outside into the graveyard. Hot and close, sun flitting in and out of billowy cloud. Lunched sitting on the grass, sheltered from the wind. Had bread, good stuff it was, the last of the lettuce and fish paste and Yeastrel, half an orange each.

Trucked down Honey Pot Lane from Gaer Hill (old spelling) and camped in wood-land in Witham Park, tucked away in the rhododendrons and surrounded by fox-gloves. Had a sudden terrible attack of hay fever which I don't normally suffer. Madhead fished around in his bag for a Contac 400 which contains belladonna. It stopped me sneezing and my nose from running and later zonked me out. Madhead went somewhere for water and I collected firewood. I brought back a decent pile and dropped it down. It was covered all over with huge wood ants, millions of the fuckers all running all over my jumper and down my trousers. Yag! Get 'em off me! Panic over, and the wind getting up so we build a fire and cook right away. Rice, lentils, potatoes, cheese. Very delicious. Had tea and slumped into the tent where Madhead is drawing a picture and I'm writing this diary.

Looking at the map I think Gaer Hill might be on the big leyline that connects Stonehenge and Glastonbury Tor. Got the pecks and ate sugar sandwiches like children. Crashed out early after writing to my brother Les and to Russ.

2022

Madhead: When we were there fifty years ago, Gaer Hill and its surroundings was another one of those mysterious places seemingly untouched by time (progress?). And, as with most rural churches I've visited since then, in St Michael's there was an almost overwhelming fustiness. Unfortunately, it stopped being a church in 2001 and I think it's now a private dwelling; the ever-marching gentrification and heathenisation of the countryside. I kind of hope it's still fusty.

The Somerset Arms in Maiden Bradley has now become a (yawn) gastropub called the (yawn again for extra effect) *Bradley Hare*. I'm livid. Bleedin' gentrifibleedincation again. Bah!

Roger shaped space: How many times did I, curious young explorer, walk into a church, and feel disappointed that I couldn't connect with that mishmash of strange symbols? Always wanted to take all that out, pews and crucifixes and pulpits and all, and begin again. The something I sought was sometimes there, in those old sacred spaces - me, or us, sitting there quietly feeling the feeling.

I like the damp Bible in that church, like it's turning to water, turning to earth, turning to the elements, like we were I guess.

"Earth water fire and air, met together in a garden fair, put in a basket bound with skin, if you answer this riddle you'll never begin..." *

* *"Koeeoaddi" There* from the 1968 album *The Hangman's Beautiful Daughter* by The Incredible String Band.

As for the hallucinatory cathedral of LSD, hardly repeated doses, a handful of times then something in me said no, I don't trust you.

Something more humble, less grand. One thing I remember from then: the recognition, the trust, scattered tribes finding the way home, conspiring - breathing together. Sometimes, from unexpected directions, or unexpected people.

Squash: Maybe it's just me, brought up an atheist, a socialist and a republican, but I had never found churches to be spiritually uplifting. They seemed dead and joyless as though life was a burden to be endured, suffocated in their own history and anaesthetised by dull hectoring sermons and authoritarian ritual. Until what happened the next day (wait and see).

Seeing what he wrote, I think I must've taken LSD more often than Roger. I tried to count the number of trips once and think it might have been around 20, maybe more. I found the experience incredibly illuminating but increasingly exhausting and, over time, more alienating. The trouble with acid was that it was still going strong long after you weren't which left you tired and edgy and feeling scruffy and dowdy after the brilliance wore off. But I wouldn't want to have missed that intense 18 month period of tripping for the insights it gave into the magical nature and strange reality of being alive.

I know now that, apparently, the universe is silent, colourless and odourless and that all these sensations are provided to you by your brain interpreting vibrations of energy to enable you to "make sense of the world". On LSD you can witness and feel these processes as they occur. Once, lying on my back gazing up at the sky through trees, I felt my vision form on the curved retina screen *inside my head*. So that I was no longer "looking out" but was constructing the sight of the world from inside myself. An interesting, if disturbing, recognition of what's really going on. Or you may occasionally soar into "white light" in which your ego dissolves and you are immersed in the cosmic dance of pure energy in which you realise that everything, including you, is part of a great shining Oneness. I had many joyful and spiritual experiences on acid as well as an unnerving deeply introspective one. It changed the way I saw and beheld the world, that's for sure.

Holy shit! What happened?

This is Whit Sunday, the Christian celebration of the Pentecost when the Holy Spirit came down and enflamed the hearts of the apostles. Hmm. Let's see what cosmic weirdness happened on this day to our spiritual questors, here on the crossroads of ley-lines and new and old gods.

From the diary:

Lay in after a really long sleep, bombed out on Contac 400. Sleep filled with many confused dreams, my brain working overtime at night to make up for the tranquil days. Made our breakfast muesli which was as delicious as ever. Madhead, good old thing, going outside into the woods later in the cold blowy grey to make a cup of tea. I got up and went up the hill through the woods to the first house for water. Nice lady in there has moved up from Penzance last year. All cosy she was and full of fun. Had a grinning chat with her. She gave me spring water and yesterday's Daily Mirror. I dug on the Norwegian looking pines and misty hills view on the way back, amazed that you can get Nordic scenery in snug Somerset.

Back at the tent we read every word of the paper, feeling weird to read about the world going on somewhere out there without us watching or caring. Lunched late on brown bread, Yeastrel, fish paste and half an orange each. As this was a leisurely Sunday we decided to rouse ourselves for 3 o'clock Evensong at St Michael's and All Angels on Gaer Hill cos we liked the isolated church on its windswept crest. Expecting little. The service had just started when we got there, us having stopped a while to dig the foxgloves and generally farting about.

The tiny church service was sparsely attended, a sprinkling of old ladies, the odd old gent in a hat here and there. Cold and dreary as usual, vicar droning in that weird deadly Christian cadence. We sat at the back, I'm looking around and daydreaming how nice it would be to live here and spend a little time and money on brightening up the peeling walls and varnishing the mildewed pews and generally injecting some life into the place. Maybe if I am ever rich … The Irish vicar started his sermon, droning on about how the Anglican and Roman churches could never be reconciled and unite – yawn – even he seemed bored by his own words.

But then something very strange and special happened. All of a sudden he had dumped his notes and went off on some mad omnidirectional mystical tirade, clearly not knowing where it might lead. Madhead and I were sitting at the back like beacons of unreality, breaking his routine of a round of dispiriting Sundays. He clocked us, he clicked on us. He lit up. He became animated and his words grew and grew louder and ever more powerful. As I listened there was a tingling rising up my spine, making the hair on the back of my neck stand up and popping pop pop pop in my mind. He was saying that church had got boring cos everyone knew what to expect and that's what they got but if they went not knowing what to expect like the apostles at Pentecost, or like the young people going to Glastonbury (Madhead and I exchanged looks - how did he know?) who go there not knowing what will happen, then maybe the fire of the Holy Spirit would come down and move them. He said it's a warning to you all - ANYONE COULD BE TOUCHED BY THE FLAME AT ANY TIME - in the church or out, it makes no difference. You should be prepared for the flame of the Pentecost to come down and for the Holy Spirit to BURN YOU UP. The church should adjust itself to THE VERITABLE VOLCANO OF SPIRITUAL ERUPTION AMONGST THE YOUNG. Holy shit, this was good stuff. He's waving his arms about and shouting now. The old ladies look a bit alarmed, cringing and cowering back in the pews, this was not the thing, not the thing at all. You don't expect to be harangued on a dull Sunday afternoon in church. When his rant drew to an end he looked sort of shocked and singed as though he'd unwittingly plugged himself into God's mains cable. It was all very moving to see and had quite a profound effect on us, but not as much as it seemed to have on him. Something unusual happened in there. Something big and meaningful and challenging between him and us.

More and more on this walk we seem to be attracted to the churches in the villages and in the remote wild but this is the first time I had ever been deeply affected by one. I like the architecture and the building materials and the craftsmanship and you can see that churches were the very centre of life - apart from the christenings, weddings and funerals, they were often the only communal spaces – and they were always open, you could always go inside, escape the tiring heat of summer. But on our walk we were looking to connect to something that pre-existed the religion of the crucified man-god. I still didn't like the Christian church but out here you can see and feel the way Christian churches were screwed down on the head and heart of the pagan faiths that went before. Churches built on the ancient sites. The Christian calendar and saints' days imposed on the old ways and astronomical feast days. This Whitsun and Pentecost malarkey, a movable date, was partially a conversion and cunning suppression of Beltane or, more probably, the celebration of the pagan summer goddess Flora.

Anyway, good old vicar. We told him at the church door how much we dug the sermon. He still looked a bit shot away by it all, like he was smouldering. We left more jubilant than we entered. He had spoken to us, understood our spiritual quest, seeking something we knew not what. We didn't expect that.

Back at Saffron Cottage we made a cup of tea and I went to my diary to try to get down some of what had just occurred. There's some bird around here that zooms off into the air on the rhythm of Hawkwind's "Silver Machine". Oh yeah, that vicar said about the church being full of Tired Tims and Weary Willies. Far out. We did the crossword in the paper and got outside again for making the dinner – mashed potatoes and lentils, carrots and hiziki, miso, bread. Had a little rap and more tea. Heard an owl hooting which put me in weird mind of a poem that starts "Owl hoot you nanny beard" which I don't know if it is a poem or something I dreamt that just runs round in my brain. Just going to write to our old friend Cabbage by flickering candlelight cos we've been talking about him and I like him a lot. Madhead just said "what time do ants go to bed?" We already in bed. No sleep. Hay fever again. Sore throat. Raw eyes. Blocked nose. Cough. Cak.

2022

Madhead: I think that was the only time in my life that I enjoyed, and was moved by, a sermon. I'd been a churchgoer from age 11 as a prerequisite to joining the 45th St Giles Reading scout group, and had also been a server for about six or seven years. I must have heard hundreds of sermons during that time but the one on Gaer Hill was a complete knockout, although the feeling soon faded and the next time I went to a church service it was back to the humdrum and ho-hum, so I continued on my heathen way.

"Owl hoot you nanny beard" sounds like it should be the title of a Captain Beefheart album.

Roger shaped space: Hey, that old time religion, it was good enough for the vicar. It was there before everything, it's in the back of everything. Define it and it goes away. Write a book about it and it hides between the lines.

I too wonder about that vicar, perhaps he was weighed down by his religion, and his vicarious position of standing in for God, and seeing our two wild rovers it was enough to tip the wink and pull out his plug. I remember, years after our walk, Squash playing a Roy Orbison track to me and pointing out the bit where he 'went mental'.... and he did, with his voice, he just hit a note that doesn't exist and it definitely sounded like he'd blown his plug out.

Anyways, wish I'd been there, my own fault for forking off. Mind you, if I'd carried on the hay fever would have got me too. It used to reduce me to an asthmatic red bulb-eyed snot wreck monster, even with double dose antihistamine.

It just occurred to me, when we were on the Ridgeway, did we meet anybody actually walking it, like us? I just remember us plodding along with pretty much no-one else around. Does it get like the M4 now in the summer? Fibreglass walking poles like the Long Man of Wilmington? Did I read somewhere you have to queue to climb Everest these days? Interesting that Buddhist pilgrims over there don't climb sacred mountains, they walk round them.

Squash: That mad ferocious sermon actually blew my mind. It was as if the vicar was inside my head and knew everything about us. He was calling down his God on us too, the flame of righteousness seized him and he blew it our way. But, looking back, I feel now that he inadvertently plugged into something that was not of his God, but of whatever power that came before, the spirit of the land and of nature. Madhead and I must've acted like a short circuit between the two systems of belief, having been to all the wild old holy places and on and off the leyline that connects Stonehenge and Glastonbury, the leyline that his church was built on, the leyline right under his pulpit, right under his feet. That's why he looked shocked, he'd been blasted by the power of the Old Ways: how could he even know we were en route to Glastonbury? We had no packs, no walking gear, nothing to lead him to think that.

I wonder what became of him. I know what became of the church. It closed and was turned into a house: now the perfect setting for a creepy Phil Rickman novel, where the old earth magic still sparks and fizzes on special days of the year. The vicar's rant definitely added to my feeling that our Walk was something imbued with mystical importance, that it meant a whole lot more than merely putting one foot in front the other.

Roger wishes he'd been there and, in my memory, he was. I was certain he was until I knew he wasn't. And to answer Roger's question, no, we saw not one other walker in the entire duration of our adventure – which seems a bit odd now, come to think of it.

Back to earthly reality

Yesterday's unearthly connection with the Pentecostal flame, or whatever powers roam the land and sky, was just the latest injection of holy spook into our little pilgrimage. I think you could say that, by now, we had become fairly detached from the material world, apart from our ever-present hunger for food. I think of it now as us having a sort of luminous opacity, drifting as we were back and forth in time as we wandered the woods, fields and lanes of Old England, the ghosts of future past..

Anyway, that's enough of that. Monday's diary is more prosaic:

Finally got to a comfortable sleep. Woke up after bizarrest dreams. Disturbed. Feeling weary but breakfast muesli was delicious. We went back to sleep, finally getting up at 10.30, woken by chainsaws and loud bangs from Tyning Wood across the road. Neither of us can get going this morning. It's muggy. We're muggy. At last packed and out on the road. Taking the track through Tyning Wood and past Grange Farm and then on through fields to Kilmington Street. Loads of cattle berserkly galloped to the fence, bellowing their heads off. Funny, a hare ran out from its cover and they all panicked and ran away.

We scored expensive groceries in the village shop. Everything a penny dearer. We are in the time of year called the Hungry Gap when fresh food is scarce. Walked up the road and stopped for lunch sitting at the war memorial cross. Bread, lettuce, Yeastrel, fish paste. Topped off with half an orange and half a Mars Bar. I went back to the shop with the cardboard box we'd borrowed and scored some Shippam's Bloater Paste cos it made me laugh. Also a packet of Treets cos they melt in your face not in your hand. Our bodies craving sweet things all the time. Had a bitch at each other about something, money I think, then went off up the road towards Alfred's Tower. Both getting the Weary Willies and thinking about all the things we could have if we weren't doing this ascetic walk. But then we talked about lone sailors, arctic explorers, mountain climbers and other braver souls and felt better, at least we weren't in mortal danger. Probably.

Passed the remains of a cross at the head of Six Wells Bottom, part of the Stourhead estate. Walked along a huge wide lawn to Alfred's "Castle", a 160 ft high brick tower, triangular in plan, built in 1772 to commemorate Alfred the Great raising his standard against the Danes there in 878/9. Restored in 1968. An incredible eye-catcher on the ridge where the hills of Wiltshire give way to the Somerset vales. We couldn't go in, it was locked up, but even from the bottom the view over Somerset was magnificent.

We pitched camp amongst the trees to the side of the lawn and I went down the steep hill to Hilcombe Farm for water while Madhead collected firewood. I am now having a rest and a hay fever attack.

Fell asleep and woke up two hours later at 7 o'clock. We are sleeping lots, dunno why. Built a fire and fixed the grits. Rice, potatoes, carrots, miso. Mmm, unusually tasty. I'm starting to think that we might be slowly starving ourselves, day after day. Our only protein and fat are what faint nutritional remnants are in the fish paste. Oh and the odd scraps of cheese. Is the increased enjoyment of any kind of food a signal of impending malnutrition? We are both even skinnier than usual, and there was barely any fat on us to begin with.

Sat around the fire enjoying our customary tea. One of those flying things that Madhead thinks are huge bats lives in this wood. It flies overhead going croak croak like a flying toad, probably just a crazed crow or a mad raven. Little bats out hunting in the dusk too, fluttering about for insects. A chick came close on a horse, she looked fine and groovy, I wanted to have a chat with her. Now preparing for sleep near the foot of the huge tower, dedicated to Alfred "Founder of the Naval Force and Father of the English, Monarchy and Liberty" as the plaque states. There's a tiny bug in here maybe quarter of an inch long with two long waving groping feelers each longer than itself. Nice creature. Now right on the border of Somerset. I wonder how different that will be.

2022

Madhead: The Weary Willies begin. There were times when I'd get visions of fruit-cake. I could even smell fruitcake. Talk about intrepid adventurers of any kidney. I was willing to sell my soul for a single bite of fruitcake.

Having lived so long in relatively near-by Frome, I've spent a lot of time since then at, up, and around Alfred's Tower. I know it was only built in the 18th century, and is only a little bit older than the USA, but there's just something amazing about its whereabouts. Then again, most hilltops have a deep history of human toil and spiritude.

I can't wait to be reminded of what we did in Somerset, land of my fathers.

Roger shaped space: The two ascetic figures moving towards Avalon, almost on the point of hallucinating food. Wasn't Alfred the Great one of those figures of the 'olden days' embellished and embroidered to fill a void in the cultural psyche? Helped to make us the Brits who we jolly well are.

Funny the things that come up triggered by the story: one pleasant October day in 2019 I was wandering in London and found myself standing looking at the Houses of Parliament. In the sunshine it was like a giant fluted freshly baked gingerbread castle. The building referred to by Laura Kuennsberg as 'that place' as she stood on the BBC news balcony. The daily Brexit theatre was going on over the road, policemen, news teams, cameras, girls in black with clipboards, small groups of for and against, protesters chanting.

Then I heard my own voice inside say "that's my place…" and I felt a surge of grief and love and tearful sadness for this land, this island on which I stand. It quite took me by surprise. A deep love of place. But Alfred the Great didn't figure there at all. Under the tarmac: the land and Mother Earth. And all those years ago, us three then you two stepping it out on ancient paths.

Squash: I think we were getting a little bit physically and mentally worn out by now, a little tired of ourselves, a little bit hungry for company, for an injection of gaiety and frolicsome life. But we had also become spiritually dourly stalwart and persevering. The Walk was all we knew.

First venture into Somerset

When you walk everywhere the old County boundaries start to make sense. Topography changes, building styles and materials are different and place-names take on a distinctive local character. The transition from Wiltshire to Somerset was very noticeable. Gone are the long-distance ridgeways, Roman roads, drove roads, ley-lines, forest tracks and bridleways. We are now in an intricate, intimate landscape of fields, winding roads, short footpaths, short cuts, and tiny strips and pieces of woodland. No clear route towards Glastonbury shows itself so we take a zigzag through sleepy villages along quiet lanes and paths, always aiming to spend the night somewhere even slightly wooded. We have decided that we wish to approach Glastonbury Tor from the west, taking part of the same route that Joseph of Arimathea was supposed to have taken, through Street and over the bridge to the Isle of Avalon, up and over Wearyall Hill, when he planted the Holy Thorn and founded Christianity in England. This involves walking a clockwise semi-circle to the south of, and at a distance from, the Tor.

This Tuesday's diary entry:

We were visited by a heavy hoofed beast during the night, with some stamping, sniffing, snuffling and snorting. Horse, donkey, stag, unicorn, Pan, monster, aliens, unknown guardians of other mysteries? I got out of the dossbag, out of the tent and went to investigate. Looking around all I could really see was Saffron Cottage, our tent, lit up from inside by a candle, shimmering iridescent orange like the landing craft of visitors from the outer reaches of the Galaxy. Maybe it was the girl on the horse come back to bewitch us. But I could find no sign of a hoof, cloven or otherwise. It was hard to get to sleep, finally with bizarre dreams again. Seems a bit of me is having a long rethink about my childhood ...

Breakfast muesli and back to sleep until ten. Leave the tent and gear and walk down the long long hill to Bruton. Our first Somerset town. Narrow streets, a stream, The River Brue, stone bridges, stone houses, posh public schools. All nice to look at. Stopped at St Mary the Blessed Virgin for our bread and spread lunch which was complemented with chips from the little chippy, wafting its seductive salt and vinegar aroma to our famished noses. Fish paste and chip butties. Far out. Grockled round the church – must be Catholic or High Anglican, very fancy, mostly old, some newer, all on the site of an earlier Abbey. Gilded moulding behind the altar with the inscription IHS and wood carved crucifixion scene, also gilded. I still don't like churches.

Grooved around the town – there's a street called Plox and a fine stone footbridge for packhorses, a protected ancient monument, which leads up a narrow covered alley. There are loads of antique shops too, inevitable tourist trade. Scoffed ice lollies and a Mars Bar, scored bread and Barmene yeast extract (yet another Marmite substitute) and cheapo cheapo cheese scraps – 10p half a pound! Nice looking chicks in there bringing back sweet memories. Make our way back, grooving on the scent of dog-roses and just out and fragrant garden roses. Some amazing gardens with huge lupins and borders of all colours, some five pointed blue bell flowers that Madhead said were Canterbury Bells. He knows lots of flowers and I am picking up the names from him, getting interested in garden flowers as well as the wild ones I was always into, that my Aunty Magda was obsessed with. Saw our first seagulls today too, and a tiny goldcrest hopping about.

Shagged out on the last steep uphill mile (1 in 6) back to our camp at the foot of King Alfred's Tower, but got water on the way. Now resting. Later had dinner of toast and fish paste at leisure with plenty of tea to wash it down. Wrote to mum, a long letter. Being on the edge of Stourhead Parkland, managed by the National Trust, we notice the bountiful wildlife. All kinds of Pink Floyd Grantchester Meadows songbirds taking your summer mind in and out. A squirrel just ran up an oak to his drey, perched high in the top branches. Occasionally, in woods, we hear the terrible death-cries of creatures meeting their ends, probably caught by weasels, stoats and foxes – all part of the pattern … but the urge to intervene is almost overwhelming, the human desire to divide Nature into good and bad.

Today at the church in Bruton we saw a poster advertising the annual Glastonbury pilgrimage on the last Saturday in June (30th). I didn't know the Christians did this. Another overlay of pagan traditions, but why not on the solstice, and why to the ruined Abbey and not the Tor? That should be interesting. Speccy Christians going one way and hairy freaks going up the Tor. Two spiritual tribes, separated by belief.

Madhead: Bruton hasn't changed much over the years. Just a few more beardy hipster-types and a massive art gallery with all that that entails. Lots of what are known as DFLs (Down From Londons) because of the handy railway station. Nice place though. Maybe because I've got friends there who might be reading this.

The Christian pilgrimage thing is a mystery. Glastonbury Abbey is not a bit like Canterbury or Lourdes. They all go up the Tor anyway. Because it's there.

Roger shaped space:

... or separated by a belief. I always wonder if I could find a way into the Christian faith that leads somewhere that isn't just back out again.

A belief system containing more jostling belief systems.

You don't need to have a belief system to dance, and kindness leaps from the heart.

Did the Beaker people believe in beakers?

We live on a hill and do hill things. We live by the ocean and do sea things.

I just meditate every morning for no reason.

Squash: I didn't mind poking around these little towns, interesting for their history and their apparent somnambulance. During the working weekdays anyway. I imagine it could be different here on a Friday or Saturday night when the pubs kick out. I was happier out in the woods though. Our camp up by the huge tower was extremely pleasant and delightful.

PART IV

Between the Two Towers
King Alfred's Tower to Glastonbury Tor

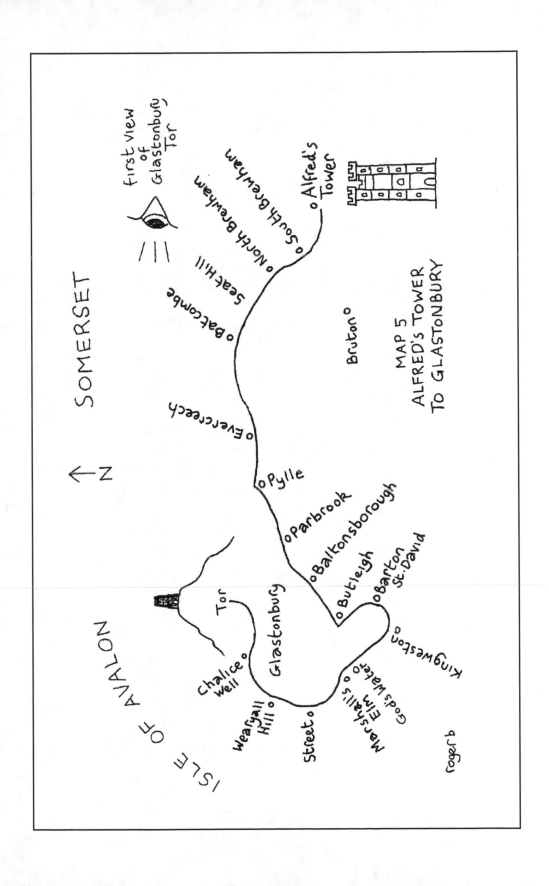

SOMERSET

ISLE OF AVALON

first view
of Glastonbury
Tor

Weymeuy
North Brewham
South Brewham

Batcombe
Seat Hill

Alfred's
Tower

Bruton°

MAP 5
ALFRED'S TOWER
TO GLASTONBURY

N

Evercreech°

°Pylle

°Parbrook

°Baltonsborough

°Butleigh

°Barton
St. David

Tor

Glastonbury

°Kingweston

Chalice°
Well

Weary all
Hill°

Street°

Marshall's°
God's Water°

roger d

Wednesday 13 June 1973

Onwards into Somerset

31 days! That's a month we've been doing this in anyone's diary. Day in, day out, always out of doors. We have our ups and downs but I'm comfortable with this way of life. Feel like I could do it forever, wouldn't need much money just a stipend of £5 a week from a kindly patron, but winter would probably put paid to that idea, kill me stone dead. Always fancied being a tramp, a vagrant, a gentleman of the road, unburdened by the weight of possessions and responsibilities, but not now, no not now, people generally being not so well disposed to the outsider.

Wednesday's diary of relaxed wandering around the byways of Somerset in the general direction westwards:

Beautiful sound sleep last night. It's the exercise what does it, up and down that bloody great hill yesterday. Got up and collected wood, made tea and ate breakfast muesli. Me feeling sad for no reason, maybe because we are leaving this favoured spot and saying goodbye to the high places. Madhead sews up the rip in his trousers and we pack up the tent and gear to get on our way. Decided to sit in the sunshine by Alfred's Tower but it's a freezing withering wind blowing so we scuttle down the hill and plunge into Somerset, take a footpath across fields to the village of South Brewham, going into St John the Baptist Church for a rest and stopping for lunch on the way. Bought some Ringer's Mixed Light and Dark tobacco for a change from Golden Virginia. Scored lentils and lollies too. These odd little village stores are always a welcome sight.

Walked up to North Brewham and took the road up to Seat Hill. From here our first distant view of …. GLASTONBURY TOR AND ST MICHAEL'S TOWER. Maybe 10 miles away. Explosion of laughter and prancing joy and hugs between us. There it is, hovering between sky and land in the distance! We could make it there today if we felt like marching but the solstice is over a week away so we will perambulate around it and creep up on it later, keeping it in view on our right-hand side. Behind us, on the ridge, you can see King Alfred's Tower, our last camp. We are now in the land between the Two Towers.

At the bottom of the hill Madhead found some hemp agrimony so he plucked a few choice leaves which are now drying out, at which point we're gonna smoke 'em, see if they do anything. The ingrained dirt on my hands is shining in the sun. At Batcombe we went into another St Mary Blessed Virgin church. It has a west tower just like the one on the Tor. I read a Ladybird book about Jesus at Galilee which is how I like my Christianity, suitable for children, full of kindness and leaving out the guilt and burning in hell stuff. Outside we bumped into the vicar, an unaccountably fierce fellow who rapped to us a bit. Think he might've suspected we were after the silver candlesticks, smelling a pagan whiff off us.

Passed through this beautiful moneyed honeyed village and are now sitting in a field by a wood at Westcombe where I'm suffering again with hay fever. Each attack getting worse as the pollen-filled air cools and floats down to earth. Yag. Madhead said he heard elves tinkling bells in the wood last night and I dreamt beautiful music. Fed. Lentils, spuds, carrots, miso, old manky cheese. Followed by tea and a smoke of the hemp agrimony which had the usual effects of spurious drug highs - light-headedness, dizziness and faint nausea.

No tent tonight, lying out digging the nearly full moon, in the full blast of night.

2022

Madhead: Sleeping under the stars is the best thing ever. It's what wild animals do if they don't live in holes. And, because it's a natural state, it's almost like being a naturist, I expect.

That first sight of the tor is a crystal-clear memory which I re-enact every day from the end of my drive. It's pretty much the same, only a lot closer.

The Christian thing has bugged me for years. There are "Christians" who seem to go to church just to be seen to be going to church, but their political views are anything but Christian as I understand it. That's why I left. That, and the lure of sex, drugs and rock 'n' roll of course.

Roger shaped space: Ah, the view of the Tor. I first saw that view in 1970 hitch hiking towards Glastonbury from Bath with my friend Roy (whose rucksack was a brown gabardine buttoned up with each end knotted with rope so it looked like a torso). Went into the only pub that served hippies, the Rifleman's Arms, and it was absolutely heaving with very hairy folk. You couldn't move for the grinning hairiness of it all. The local scrumpy was very strong and I'm sure we partook of a joint containing the dried leaves of the Holy Thorn, which probably had the same effect as the hemp agrimony described above, but hey. Then we somehow pitched our drunken orange tent* in the dark on the side of the Tor in torrential rain, falling all over the place, and with two girls who'd made the mistake of asking us if we knew of anywhere they could crash. We were woken up at dawn by a stream of water rushing through the tent. Found a level campsite on the disused railway in town the next afternoon where we were pelted with green Somerset apples by bellowing local lads on the other side of the hedge. This was only part one of our welcoming initiation however, as the next morning a line of severed chicken feet greeted us as we crawled out of the tent.

* there is a possibility that this could have been Saffron Cottage?

Squash: Could that really have been Saffron Cottage that Roger had in 1970? My memory is that we three bought it new, cheap and on a whim. But my memory can be a big fat phony at times, even though it would swear on its life that whatever it decides is true. It has yet to explain to me why so many of my memories are in the form of a third-party view. In other words, I see most of my memories *with me in them,* like a photograph or film, not as if I'm looking at events through my own eyes. For example I can envisage Madhead and me cavorting and laughing and hugging each other on that hilltop. I know that my memory has been playing fast and loose with the past, putting an epic slant on things with its egotistical idea of me as a leading actor in the drama of my own life. I wonder why it does that.

Anyway, yes, the first sight of Glastonbury Tor was exhilarating. After walking for 31 days suddenly the end was within our grasp. But it had come too soon. Unbelievable as it might seem, we hadn't walked slowly enough. A whole week to fritter away before the solstice.

Creeping up on Glastonbury through the towns, villages and hamlets of Somerset

Thursday diary:

So much for sleeping under the moon. Bloody freezing and damp. Awake most of the night, really cold. Saw a UFO limp slowly across the sky. Orange light creeping soundlessly over. We chose our site badly last night and had to get up and move across the field to catch the early morning sun to warm up and dry out. Very pleasant, warmth creeping back into stiff bones, eating breakfast.

Took the road through Stony Stratton to Evercreech, glimpsing Glastonbury Tor again in the distance on the way. Now that we have seen it, it is as though it is always with us, a presence even when not visible. The magical mystical Isle of Avalon, where our quest will end.

Once there at Evercreech I needed a crap so went into the Bell Inn had me a crap on the luxury of a bog seat and then we had halves of bitter outside in the sun. Sat in the churchyard of St Peter's with jackdaws roistering about and had our lunch, manky cheese sandwiches with peppery nasturtium leaves which we swiped from the pub's tubs. It was getting hotter and hotter so we lay around an hour or so, then we go into the church to cool off. Usual Somerset build, great west tower in stone, solid, stolid, sturdy, unmoving, lifeless. The 10-peal of bells here being the famous ones heard on the wireless for many years. I don't care, still don't like churches. Soul crushing. Authority. Just leaving Evercreech we espied a chip shop. Temptation won. We can resist anything except the temptation to put stuff in our mouths.

Then down the road towards Pylle, blazing sun, raging hay fever, air full of pollen and dust. Find a sadly dead fox cub, recently killed, very beautiful, just a-lying in the road. Shame on Man and a pox on his cars. Lay down in a field for a sunbathe and more suffering. I swear you can see hazy clouds of pollen rising off the field. We grooved with a caterpillar who looked like Dougal. He wasn't eating mushrooms. Yet.

Crossing the A37 at Pylle – fast, noisy and dangerous to us slow moving critters – and then stopping at the shop for ice creams. On again to Pylle village with its lovely-looking church dedicated to Thomas a Beckett, bearing its dedication on a painted plaque outside, over the gate. On the door handle it said "a prayer with their hands they have sung". A Craftsmen's Guild church, full of the best handmade ironwork and woodwork. Madhead learnt here that St James is the patron saint of pilgrims, his plaque being silver and blue representing high ideals and chivalry. That's us! Unfortunately he had his head cut off for his trouble, St James not Madhead. Gulp. On the wall a plate made from clay dug from the Tor, inscribed "England's Holiest Erthe". Far out. Maybe that's what we've been looking for, maybe that's what we are coming to, maybe we'll take root there. Who knows?

Lay down outside on the grass, where I fell asleep. Madhead waking me up to my worst ever attack of hay fever – dizziness, weakness, raw nose and throat, acute weary willies. Found a field just outside the village to kip in where Madhead fell asleep drowsy summer day, and I brooded among the bees and blossoms. This is a fine spot, so peaceful and flowery. Finally I went off to a house for water. Came back and collected wood, built a fire and made dinner. Rice and lentils, potato and carrot. Miso. Cheese. That put a lot back into me. Thank you God whoever you are. Relaxing at last, hay fever in abeyance. Sunset sky, streaked with red. Nice fire and Madhead's making a start on carving a pipe out of thorn wood. In Pylle church is a wooden altar cross "made without a plane". I opened the bible in there and it opened on prophecies, Isiah this time. All about the destruction of Babylon. Hmm … still waiting for that.

2022

Madhead: Babylon still hasn't fallen fifty years on. Steel Pulse thought it might in 1978 (ref. *Handsworth Revolution*) but they were wrong. The Bell at Evercreech hasn't fallen either … yet. It's now a bit of a gastro paradise although the cider is still only three quid or so per pint which is good for around here.

Most of the dead animals one finds on the road these days are either foxes or badgers. I often wonder if Farmer Giles pops 'em off with his Purdey and slings them on the road to make it look like an accident. I wouldn't put it past him.

Roger shaped space: 'I still don't like churches' you say, adding 'soul crushing' and 'authority'.

Etymology suggests *church* relates back to *kurios* master, *kuros* power.

I was just thinking about that feeling at Avebury of warmth and the village in the stones, the sun shine and the village and the kids.

The grim feeling at Stonehenge, the monoliths on the plain, hmmm.

The beauty of Salisbury cathedral yet the overtones of male religious hierarchy.

The country churches often built on old pagan sites.

Etymology of pagan relating back to country folk, rustic, heathen, of the heath.

Wouldn't the Tor actually look better without that tower on top of it? An insult to the Earth Mother. But didn't she shake her tail feathers and demolish the rest of the church leaving a perky silhouette breast as a landmark?

Approaching Avalon, the isle of the apples. Approaching Glastonbury, a right old stewpot of conflict which is just floating mist to our travellers' simple hearts.

Squash: I don't know why we visited so many churches in Somerset. They were probably inescapable, the only places you could sit in the cool for a while. And they also seemed to occupy the centre of things – you came to a place and there it was, the church. Everything else clustered about it. But the religious aspect of them failed to twang my heartstrings. They seemed of their time, a crushing presence on the rural peasantry. Probably not like that at all but I am clearly hostile to churches. I wonder why that is. To me they are the opposite of what I hold dear – joy, enthusiasm, glee, freedom, welcome, friendship, grace, respect. Dead men's bones in brick and stone.

Summer then had become drowsy and weighed down with its own fecundity, heat and dust and pollen. Only the early mornings and the evenings provided respite.

Friday – the weekend starts here!

The diary says:

Good morning! Up at five this morning after a beautiful warm sleep by the campfire, and watching the sun climbing up through the trees. Made tea in the first golden rays streaming out across the grass, stoked up the fire and woke the foolish friend. Warm early sun dragging soft mist across this field and away. Sat around warming up and later mixed the muesli. Out on the road before eight.

Light easy walk to East Pennard but the Post Office is still closed so we walk on into Parbrook, a "retired" village. A lady has a post office and a tiny shop in the hallway of her house. We wanted tobacco but she didn't have any, but she split a twenty pack of No 6 fags, ten for us, ten for her. I bet she couldn't believe her luck, a good excuse - ten ciggies for her as an act of kindness, puffing away to her heart's content. Well she couldn't very well sell them could she? Not once they had been opened. Bought two apples too, split one between us at the bottom of the road. Walked on from there along Ham Street and into nasty country hick Baltonsborough which was a disappointing, unfriendly place. It had a bad vibe for some reason we didn't understand.

The Tower on the Tor seems to be watching our every move now as we encircle it. It's creeping closer and getting bigger.

Scored our meagre groceries at the village. Country people must eat worse food than townies. No fresh fruit and veg. I asked for a cucumber and the shopkeeper she said "this is the country you know". Well bugger me! Amusing, eh? Also had to make do with sliced prepacked Hovis Roundy bread, most of which we ate with our lunch in the local churchyard, St Dunstan's. Walked to Butleigh, fucked up on our intended sleeping place in Parkwood and a meadow was out of the question because the hay fever was nearly bursting my brain. So into the little town we went. Scored bread and dates and ices each at the shop and went to the church, St Leonard's, which has a one handed clock and is next to Butleigh Court, an amazing building, all chimneys and turrets but in a too-close and odd juxtaposition with the church. Turns out it has no roof and is a derelict. The stonework of the structure looked in good condition though.

We eat our tea here, muesli and a sandwich each with cucumber from the local shop in Butleigh. It seems that cucumbers do exist in the countryside after all. Went for a dull walk around and ended up back at the church, not knowing what to do. So, usual remedy, off to the inn we go, the Rose and Portcullis, where we have two pints of bitter each and play all these amazing old sounds on the jukebox, stuff like "Badge" and "What a Bringdown" by Cream and "Beck's Bolero" and "Albatross" and "Nights in White Satin".

Back to St Leonard's where there is a youth club in progress in the church room, so we munch another sandwich and a Mars bar and groove on the action! Reminders of younger youth club days. One chick, more mature than the others, very lovely, stands out from the horde, doing nothing, arms akimbo, bored with the chaotic British Bulldog childishness. Her posture suggesting she would welcome some excitement. I idly wonder if she would like to get passionate in a field with a dirty starving hippy tramp. Probably not. I ask her (no, not that) and she in turn goes asks the lady if we can have some coffee from their refreshment table. Just an excuse to talk to her. We get the coffee. Thank you. That lovely girl could have had me if she'd played her cards right and had hidden her indifference. Oh well.

Club grinds to a halt and we go outside and crash out by an old tree stump in the field by the church. The tent has become redundant, we can just fall over and kip anywhere. The nearly full moon of last night has fattened to a perfect circle. Tonight is as light as a Saturday afternoon. Well, almost.

2022

Madhead: I'll have the world know that nasty country hick Baltonsborough has become a fashionable, "in" and happening place to be now that I live there, Teapot Lane, off Ham Street, and with a wonderful view of the Tor, used to be called Worms Lane. Make of that what you will. The original village shop closed a while ago but has since been replaced by a shop/bakery/café which is a Mecca for cyclists and grumpy old men. I ought also to mention that my wife is on the Parish Council.

In Butleigh, the "Rose and Port" as she is known, had a refit three years ago but has recently closed. Probably because those tunes were still on the jukebox.

Roger shaped space: Coming to the endnotes of my footnotes now as the Tor looms for you. The notepads of the footpads. All those days on the byways and pathways leading to the zero of just being human, tis all it is. Man goes walkabout, eyes peeled, and the journey is the destination.

I like this choice of the long curved arrival, skirting round, coming in to roost, the magic hill on the right of the gaze, not straight ahead. It's like a respectful way for the weary pilgrim to arrive.

Squash: From Wikipedia: *Butleigh Court, (1845) which was abandoned for many years and has now been brought back into use, is noted for its interesting architecture including the tall carved chimney stacks, which are all different. Local legend has it that the family was cursed to die out within a hundred years, which subsequently happened.*

From the Welcome to Glastonbury website:

The Grenvilles became Lords of the Manor in 1738 and in the following years a new house was built taking in land from the churchyard and causing a legend to grow that because bones had been disturbed the house would go in a hundred years. The family has gone but the Court has been restored and now houses four families.

I read somewhere that the building of the 1845 replacement Butleigh Court also interrupted a ley line which brought added misfortune.

The nearer we got to the end of our journey the more the thrill diminished. You could feel the normal workaday world waiting in the wings, beckoning us in. Probably why we skirted round the Tor to delay our arrival. It was still nice though, exploring all these little places on our complicated route but more like a little walk in the country than adventurous footsteps.

A little conflict over some water

Our pilgrims' progress is resolute if slow. Creep creep creeping up inch by inch and minute by minute on the Tor and on the solstice like a pair of holy hairy expectant fools. We have a little contretemps with water-supremacists and suffer a show of hostility towards hippies. All the while the Tor is watching us as we circle south and south-west, under its gaze.

Saturdiary:

I wake up early, early morning bare grey first light, not cold, but I can't breathe. Throat constricted, chest wheezing, can't get enough air in. About an hour I lay there working carefully at slow shallow breathing. Something tells me to stay still, stay calm, that if I panic I'm finished. Hay fever, asthma, bronchitis, fuck knows, looming death. I really thought I would die, suffocating in the encompassing presence of air. Horrible and very frightening. Finally must've dropped off again cos woke up again at 6.30. Sun just climbing through the trees, so I get up potter about have a crap and ablute, breathing lightly and wheezily. Mix the muesli adding sliced apple for a luxury treat. Wake Madhead up, eat, smoke a roll-up, cough like fuck, pack and take our leave of Butleigh, the centre of the Temple of the Stars. Walk up to the woods at Wickham's Cross where we stash our packs in the hedge, hiding them under Madhead's dark green coat.

Long long hot walk to Barton St David, the village that is supposed to be laid out in a representation of a dove in the Zodiacal Temple. We pass the Dove Centre of Creativity which sounds far out but is probably shit. We didn't go in. Don't know why. Sounds a bit too worthy to me. On into the village, ice creams, scored malt loaf and spring onions and oranges. Cooled off in the nice simple church of St David's which has a very unusual octagonal tower and an obelisk war memorial in the grounds. Read a lump of the Gospel according to St John, Jesus saying you should love one another.

Presently a woman comes in to do the flowers so we go outside to lunch. Now sweating in the midday sun. This place pleasantly peaceful, worthy of the dove.

Walked to Kingweston across the fields. A street of what appears to be lined with abandoned and boarded up houses. Curious. The manor house still in use. The Post Office is closed so we have to walk back along the road to Wickham's Cross for our bags and on past the monument down the hill to a little wood near Marshall's Elm. We stash the bags again in the hedge of a field with a fantastic view of the Tor and go off in search of tobacco. Finally reaching Elms Inn where we guzzle three pints each and scoff pickled eggs. Stagger back half-pissed and giggle-bound. We espy a tap on a stand-pipe, mounted on the stone wall at the entrance to a little camping ground. This would save disturbing someone in a house so we're just about to fill our water-bottle when an angry lady bustles over and says

"Don't touch that water"

"Why, what's wrong with it?"

"There's nothing wrong with it. It's for our campers only."

"Why?"

"Because it is"

"Well, if I knocked on your front door and asked you for water, would you refuse me?"

"I expect I would, yes."

"Well then you'd be the first person in a month's travelling who would. I think I'm gonna take it anyway."

"Right, I'll get my husband to you two."

The bottle just fills up when hubby comes out, waving his arms about in an aggressive manner, trying to shoo us away like we're angry wasps around his jampot. This man does not seem to realise that he is dealing with holy fools, mighty noblemen of the road that have trod the highways and byways of Old England to arrive here.

"Go on get out, just because it's a lady that asks you not to take the water, you ignore her."

"Calm down. Even if YOU had asked me not to take it I would've anyway. Water is a man's right. I've walked 150 miles to get here and no-one has yet refused me water."

"It's not a man's right. I have to pay to pump it up here, it's for our campers and it's our water."

"They may be your pipes and pump but it's God's water that falls freely from the sky to everyone under it. You can't own water."

Lady, aggressively: "where are you camping tonight?"

"That's our business. Not here that's for sure."

Man: "go on get out, never step a foot in here again".

Lady "I know, you're camping on the Tor where the gods give you energy or something".

"That would be a damn sight more than you would give us".

Man "go on get out, take your water with you, never step foot in here again".

"Fair enough. You can have it all back when I've finished with it. I'll even deliver it personally."

Walk away. It does make you wonder. A big bringdown really, stupid disagreement, I feel bad now, for getting bolshy. We could've easily gone somewhere else for water. But … but … meanness with water? Just four pints of water, four little pints of water from his little water tap? I shouldn't have got feisty, it's only water. Four little pints of water in this big old wet land of ours. Fuck them anyway.

Back to our bags and our field, collect wood, make a fire and cook dinner. The Tor is hanging above us, lit up by the setting sun. White rice now, the brown having all gone. It's not the same, it has no soul. Lentils, potatoes and carrots, spring onion stalks, miso, cheese. Tea.

We are very close to Glastonbury now, can feel it crackling. Can't delay our arrival much longer. Crash out in the field by the hedge.

2022

Madhead: Ha! The legend of *That's Not Your Water, It's My Water* is a great one for the telling. Apart from public bogs, it was the only time we didn't ask someone for water and what a palaver ensued! I never ask for water from anyone with a flagpole displaying the Union Flag now as a matter of principle.

My wife and I went to the Dove Centre a few years ago as part of the Somerset Arts Trail. It was disappointing. Very expensive works and very offhand people. We like to support local artists when we can, but the ones at the Dove didn't seem to be that bothered, so we didn't bother either.

Roger shaped space: Yeah, well, prejudice. No hippie weirdos with long unkempt hairdos.

I wonder if the man stood in his kitchen waving his arms around first to get up to the right speed, like a helicopter before take-off, like working up to his 'high horse' level, then stepped out of his door whirling, fully prepared, but not prepared to meet you.

It's funny that about Glastonbury, despite everything, there is something about the place. You can feel it crackling.

17 years later I had a similar whirling arms encounter when I put up a worse for wear ex-army bell tent in the middle of a jam-packed family campsite somewhere near Ambleside. I had my family with me. I'd just banged in the last tent peg and adjusted the guy ropes and looked round and there was the campsite owner striding towards me with his arms whirling furiously: "What the HELL do you call THAT!" Our friendly neighbours not-to-be who were very welcoming of our eccentric selves watched in bemusement as I just reversed the process and packed the tent away into the boot of our worse for wear car without saying a word, apart from "You want us to go then? That sounds very calm and Zen but actually I was so

knackered that day it was just easier to turn it into theatre. The whole show lasted about 30 minutes. I should have charged them.

Squash: I don't know what put a bee in her bumhole. Or who wound up his helicopter.

Must've been looking out the window and spotted us two water-wanters and freaked out at the sheer bloody cheek of it. The giggling probably didn't help.

Doesn't excuse my snarkiness though, not really. Could easily have got water somewhere else. I give hippies a bad name. Taking water from a tap without so much as a by-your-leave.

This is it folks, the day we have been waiting for, the day our happy hippie heads finally enter Glastonbury! Their joy was unbounded, their goal attained

You will notice that we are a few days short of the summer solstice. Unfortunately your reporter seems to have quit completing the diary as soon as Glastonbury was reached. A diary is a tiresome thing to compile, as each day as it is lived seems to be of little moment or import, its value, if any, lies way off in the uncertain future when the dying day's prosaic words might take fire and re-ignite memories, seen from the perspective of an old man looking back at his young self and his kith with wonder and a measure of bewilderment. Ah yes, it all comes back to me. Well, some of it anyway.

So this is the last entry informed by the diary. Tomorrow, as an epilogue, I will attempt to offer some probably poorly remembered fragments of what occurred in the following days while our heroes tooled around in Glastonbury until the dawn and day of the solstice had passed.

From this midsummer Sunday diary:

Bad wheeze waking again, this hay fever is doing my nut in. Didn't really get off to sleep until the first creeping light spread over the land, might've dozed a bit. No burst of sunrise, just grey light slowly seeping in and the day emerging. The Tor looks fantastic from here, towering over us and the field we are sleeping in. Madhead wakes me with a bowl of muesli. Whispers to look. Quiet now. Badger cubs playing in the grass not 15 feet away, seemingly unconcerned by two human chrysalids that appeared overnight. Light a twiggy fire and make tea. Doze again in the dossbag.

On the road at ten after stitching tears in my jeans. It's turned into a hot and cloudy close day. Glastonbury Tor looming to our right, its shape shifting continually as we move west. We are moving like the rim of a wheel with the Tor as its hub, except that we are actually spiralling ever closer to the centre, like winding ourselves up on a Maypole. On we go into Street, a busy workaday sort of town, and over Pons Perilis Bridge and so onto the Isle of Avalon of legend. Over the great hump of Wearyall Hill in the footsteps of Joseph of Arimathea, past the holy thorn that immediately grew and blossomed from the staff that he stuck in the ground. WE MADE IT. WE ARE HOME! We are in Glastonbury.

Quick exhausted lunch of malt loaf and dates, a drink of metallic water from the Chalice Well then up to magical Tor top St Michael's Tower. Lots of freaks milling about. Meet two guys who introduce themselves as Gimli and Legolas. "Really?" we ask. "Yes, we changed our names". As you would expect one is tall and slim, the other is short and stout. We thought how funny it would be if the short one was Legolas and the tall one was Gimli. That made us laugh. Mind you, they probably thought we were a bit weird when we introduced ourselves as Squash and Madhead. This all added to the strange feeling we had that we were the only ones up here who were real, probably because we've been together on our own for so long that everyone else seemed like actors.

Truck off to hippie Abbey Café in its odd location facing the car-park. It's still nice as it ever was, music and freaks, massive bowl of muesli on the counter into which folk dip. New mural on the wall. Tea. Guy who runs it says to Madhead he's never seen two people who looked so high. We were too. High and Mighty. Weary travellers, hard and thin, browned by the outdoors, carrying spiritual overload, wide eyes flashing dangerously. He said we shimmered and were almost transparent. The town seemed weird to me, somehow disjointed and badly focused. Something must have happened to us during our walk. Wandering around the place we bump into Patch which is amazingly good fortune, just perfect to find a loving friendly face, giving a point to our aimlessness. She takes us to the house she lives in, along the road from the foot of the Tor at the top of the town, the house of a lady named Nancy. Also staying there was John who we met when we came down last year in the Magic Bus and who reminds me of Boromir.

Glastonbury sure does it to you though; we start to feel more comfortable. We smoke some dope with John and talk about Carl Jung's book *"Man and his Symbols"*. Jung was an eminent man in a suit and tie trying to make intellectual and rational sense of our innermost irrational and mystical selves. We talk especially about the archetypal figure of the Wanderer. Wanderers are characterized by movement, absence from society and home, engaging with wilderness, limited visibility, and the ability to be unattached to the outcome of things. Hahaha, sounds familiar.

Suddenly I don't like being indoors, feel hemmed in. I long to get outside to the trees, the ground, the sky, the sun, the moon and stars, the campfire, the billy-can, the birdies and beasties that go about their business around and about you. Back to nature I want but we kip on Patch's floor instead. Tomorrow will be a different sort of day for us.

2022

Madhead: Ah yes. Glastonbury is still one of those places where you bump into people and friends when you least expect to. I suppose it goes with the territory in a manner of speaking. It was definitely weird sleeping under a roof for the first time in six weeks. As you say, there was a sense of claustrophobia, but it soon wore off after a bit of spliff and I slept that first night like a baby.

The Abbey Café is sadly no longer with us, but there are many look-alike places around nowadays. I think the owner was called Andy and he had a massive motor-bike so was quite the cool dude.

Roger shaped space: I like what you say about keeping a journal, and the bouncing time span. Remembering the teaching from the little green bug.

Arriving, a step over the threshold, a now useless staff stuck into the ground to sprout and the journey is over and the journal is already complete and compiled maybe. Things open out from the winding path you took into a wide field of hellos to say to Glastonbury, the apple of your eyes for all those days and nights. I'll leave it at that as a footnote man, knowing there is an epilogue to chew over. One thing about reading your journal has been the many sub plots and storyettes (often of anything but the Walk) that fluttered out of this wild and unpredictable (for me) thing called memory.

Squash: We arrived shimmering and vaguely transparent and high and almost not of this world. A feeling that stayed with me for quite some time. It seems astonishing now that we never gave a single thought to what we were going to do when we reached Glastonbury. Thank the Fates for Patch showing up, a good welcoming woman.

The last few days to and beyond the Solstice

It's a well-worn saying that the journey is more important than the arrival. There's something in that and in our case the journey was a wide-eyed experience of wonder and learning. But without a destination a journey means little and can descend into aimless wandering. It was a cause of joy and achievement for us to arrive in Glastonbury after 35 days living in the open air on a frugal diet and with just the basic necessities to sustain us. I'm not sure what we expected when we finally arrived but certainly we hoped for some sort of tangible magic to occur as a climax to our quest. That didn't really happen. But looking back I can see that magic, in its various forms, was with us all the way.

As for Glastonbury, the truth is we experienced more magic the previous year when we drove down in a big orange seatless minibus with the Cosmic Capers Club, having visited Avebury and Silbury Hill en route. What Roger called a Van-Bang. Sleeping in the bus down Cinnamon Lane we all shared the same dream of huge megaliths flying through the air, tumbling and rolling as if weightless but guided by unseen hands. However Glastonbury is always a great place to be. The Tor and the ruined tower imbue the place with a powerful energy.

Having arrived in Glastonbury yesterday (Sunday) our wanderers have three days to kill before the summer solstice. Kill time we must have, we had thumbs to twiddle after all. The trouble is that, without the diary entries, I have no clear memory of what we did do, just a few disconnected fragments in no particular order, a jumbleation of events. Perhaps we were dazed and dazzled by the bright lights of the bustling metropolis after all those days in the windy air. Maybe Madhead has better recollection than me. I do know we were on the chilly Tor at dawn on 21 June 1973, to mark the sunrise on the summer solstice. There were lots of freaky people there. There was no clear sunrise, the day didn't break, it just slid in greyly and gradually. After a while the crowd dispersed.

Remembered fragments:

Within hours of arriving at Glastonbury I contracted a terrible case of the shits that continued for three weeks. That hippie Abbey Café, great place as it was, was probably none too hygienic. Mind you, Madhead somehow contrived to work there, for the nice couple who ran it, and he didn't get the shits. He might even have got paid, I can't remember. Oh and when I say shits, I really mean shits. About every half hour I had to find a bog to squirt burning liquid into. Patch's house was none too clean either when I think about it. Of course we were no longer cooking our own meals, I guess we ate at Patch's house sometimes and we always had breakfast muesli at the Abbey Cafe. At the time I thought that the massive communal bowl of muesli on the counter was a wonderful idea. People paid their money and just helped themselves to it but maybe a few filthy fingers went into that bowl, including mine.

While Madhead was helping out in the café, for free food I think, myself unable to eat properly, I spent some time by the chain-link fence between the car-park where the café was and the school playground across the way talking to the little kids. I was having little fun-filled chats with them when they excitedly spilled out at playtime. The public toilets were in the car-park and, owing to my over-enthusiastic bumhole, I rarely risked going too far away. They were lovely lively kids anyway, asked me all sorts of questions to which I gave appropriate daft answers. I went further down the way to see where the railway station used to be and thought how short-sighted it was that another, albeit relatively short-lived, track to Glastonbury had been axed. It was a sad sight, the station platforms and canopies now part of a timber yard, the rails lifted, the permanent way destroyed.

I explored the town and the Abbey, walked over Chalice Hill and spent a lot of time sitting on the bench on the High Street outside St John's watching the world go by and clenching my anus.

We must have stayed at Patch's house, kipping on the floor I guess. But one weird night, most likely the 20th, Solstice Eve, when the town had filled with freaks, we slept in our dossbags on the floor of a hall, must have been parish rooms or something, upstairs, just off the High Street that had become like a refugee station for loads of itinerant hippies. Patch was with us. There was a little kitchen filled with frantic activity to feed soup and bread to the steady stream of people arriving, looking for shelter. The weather had been cold and dreary and everyone looked pinched and worn. We had bagged a place on the floor in a corner of the big room near the door as I had to be in quick reach of the bog.

Late on as everyone was settling down to sleep the double doors burst open and a gang of drunken local young men burst in, hollering insults about dirty hippies and threatening violence to everyone in the room. It seems these fine specimens of fuckwittedness were not keen on seeing "their" town being invaded by a band of psychedelic gypsies. The ringleader, a vicious looking hard-man in the regulation clean white shirt and suit jacket, could get no response from anyone and was trying to rouse himself to further rage by shouting and swearing into the dim, hippy-filled twilight of the hall while his peanut-brained supporters hovered menacingly behind. Eventually he lifted a metal dustbin over his head and hurled it into the middle of the room with an angry roar and a clang of metal. I don't know if it hit anyone but there was fear and incipient panic in the room. What a wanker. Madhead and I were lying to one side, fingering our sheath knives, and thinking self-defence. I have often thought of that occasion and wish that I had had the presence of mind to start the Om. That would have spread around the room like wildfire. We could've Ommed the bastard into submission to the Ultimate Reality. Hey ho, never mind. Maybe next time around.

We trooped up the Tor in the chill before light to welcome the summer solstice sunrise. It was blustery and bleak up there and when the dawn came it was an anti-climax. No sign of the sun, just a grey light stealing in from the East. But later that morning we had a wonderful surprise. Roger turned up and found me and Madhead and Patch sitting on the bench outside the church in the High Street. Well met indeed. He had our friend Chris with him and there might have been others.

My hay-fever had continued, but not as bad as when I nearly died of an asthma attack in that fucking field. Roger was a long-time hay-fever sufferer and explained to me about anti-histamines. I had never had hay-fever before and had no idea it could be managed with tablets like Piriton. That was a godsend and I had just enough money left to buy a pack. Now all I needed to do was stem the raving shits which were seriously not helping me regain some of the weight and vitality I had lost. Unfortunately anything I put in my mouth produced an instant and opposite reaction at the other end.

On the following Saturday my good friends Graham and Erica answered my desperate postcard plea for sanctuary and drove down from Bristol to take me to their home where they ministered unto me. The raging shits went on for three weeks. I went to the doctor's in the end and he did a blood test. When it came back all he asked was whether I had been in close proximity to cows. Well there was the licky one, the cute Jersey that seemed enamoured of me. But he didn't say any more so I was none the wiser. Maybe this was the Walk's final gift – to completely empty me in readiness for the next phase of life.

Madhead came to Bristol as well soon after and we lived together with hippie friends old and new in a shared house/commune for a while until we went our own ways following the lure of women and steered in different directions.

I was in Bristol 23 years, Madhead left Bristol a few years before me to live in Frome so part of our vague intention to settle there when we embarked on the Walk came partially true. For my part the closest I could manage was marrying a girl from Frome. Funny how it works out. Roger took his own singular path. Lived in a succession of shared houses and then on the Oxford canal on a narrowboat for years and wound up in Shropshire where he lives on in all his charismatic ways.

It would be nice to end with a summary of lessons learnt, or spiritual growth gained, or at least something profound but I reckon most people can pick the bones out of the story for themselves. The Walk showed us how constrained and prescriptive "normal" life is, separated from the wonders of Nature and the roll of the seasons, ruled by factory/office time, allowed a couple of weeks holiday. What is a longed-for holiday if not an admission that your daily life is basically shit? From that time on I was determined that the difference and separation between my working life and my home life would cease to exist, or at least be complementary. The only work I did from then on was integrated into the enthusiasms, interests and meanings of the rest of my life.

The Walk also showed us that the number of good people in the world far exceeds the number of the bad, but that the bad guys have a disproportionately greater impact on the way we have to live, the keys and the locks, the being watchful and the guarded suspicion, fear of strangers and go careful with the glee. Re-reading this story again reminds me of what a good tribe to belong to was hippiedom. For a few years it meant you had friends everywhere, friends you hadn't met yet, people on the same wavelength who would feed you, offer you a floor to kip on, share their smokes and have a laugh – no questions asked. I don't really know why that went away or where it went, that level of mutual understanding. I guess we all grew older and took on responsibilities. Still get little flashes of it, now and then.

I'm not very profound really. Apart from my love of nature, history and landscape I still mostly like sex and drugs and rock'n'roll. When I say "drugs" I include alcohol. It has always amazed me, the hypocrisy of people who drink professing to be anti-drugs. Just different ways to get out of your head and alcohol being the most personally and socially damaging of them all by a distance. I get my recharge of earth energy from my garden and my allotment and from the trees in the ground and the birds in the sky. The things that humans desire and chase seem to mean little to me. I am lucky, I'm in love with my wife (40 years and counting) and our children and grandchildren are a source of joy, pride and humour. You know the expression "get out of your comfort zone"? Well, I spent a long part of my life trying to get into one and I'm glad to say I might be just about there. It has taken me many a year but the journey has been … well, you know … pretty fucking horrendous. Hahaha. Just kidding.

I have learnt something though which I would like everyone to adopt. Be nice, be kind and quit shoving. Always try to give more than you take. That's all there is.

I have great memories of the Walk and the wonderful Ridgeway and all the monuments the Old Ones left us to puzzle over. We had a Cosmic Capers Club reunion on Glastonbury Tor on New Year's Eve 1992/3.

COSMIC CAPERS CLUB

Grand Reunion

New Year's Eve 1992-3

Glastonbury Tor

It was a breathtakingly cold frosty night, the Tor swathed in a blanket of thick freezing fog. Trudging upwards through the fog, at the very top we were amazed to emerge into a brilliantly starlit crystal clear night – just the Tower and us and a small patch of ground suspended above an endless great ocean of silent smothering fog. The ruined Tower stood bold and stark, pointing up to the zinging sparkling heavens. Magic. Roger showed up as did good friends Russ and Chris and Lou, maybe some others, but not Madhead. I got told off for leaping into the fog and disappearing down the hill but we all met up at the bottom and went into the Rifleman Arms to see in the New Year.

Madhead and I saw a lot of each other in Bristol and Roger and I visited each other for many years, sharing a new-found interest in playing Irish traditional music. I have met up with Madhead a few times more recently, the last time in Bath in 2018.

The three of us still keep in touch, mostly by email. We are all fine, happy and settled – as much as the vagaries of life allow anyway.

Madhead: This whole exercise was, for me, a means of escape. Reading was a very hard place to leave after having spent my formative years there. The Walk seemed like a good plan and, as it turned out, it was. The waking nearly every morning in a different place, becoming a stranger to even stranger people and further developing a lifelong love of nature and all her wonders was a brilliant episode. Was it only six weeks? At times it felt like we'd always lived like that – gathering firewood, eating simple but nutritious (up to a point) food, sleeping under the stars when the weather was kind enough – three, then two, souls in search of their tomorrows, having fun, murmuring philosophies to each other, stretching our legs towards the horizon. It was a good time to be alive. I'm certain we couldn't do it these days even if we were healthy and fit enough. Lighting fires everywhere? Asking for water in remote houses? I don't think so. Even the village shops have mostly disappeared.

Glastonbury was the destination but the journey was the thing. The escape.

There is still a draw to the place, and after fifty years of ageing and wearying, my former self is now a shadow and my current self sits and wonders at the many people in Glastonbury who appear to be on their way to a 70s fancy dress party. I wouldn't have it any other way.

Roger: Wrapping up with a few slightly clearer recollections, thoughts and things and things.

Ridgeway to Avebury was a connection with something wild and ancient, but Glastonbury increasingly felt like a symbol for something I didn't want to be involved with any more. I loved the place but I was getting very uneasy with the scene. I wanted out of the hippie swamp, not deeper into it and I remember this was woven into the journey somehow.

After our sad parting, I ended up going north to a different magic hill. I'd forgotten this. After being validated as a Zen monk by the Japanese girls in Inverness (see day 24) I went to a high wooded hill standing on its own just on the south west of the town centre called Tomnahurich: the hill of the fairies. It's a massive cemetery and I knew there were graves of my ancestors there, somewhere. I spent hours wandering the pathways up and up looking at headstones, until I reached the summit, and suddenly there they were in pride of place, my great great grandparents and various others, their names inscribed on marble stones on the very top of the fairy hill.

From Inverness I went up to Ross and Cromarty and over to Ullapool before returning south and made it to Glastonbury for a happy reunion with Squash and Madhead.

The circle turns, Squash and Madhead went to Bristol, I returned to the Thames Valley and lived in various houses doing various jobs, did my art degree at the infamous Hornsey College of Art and so on and so on. A lot has happened in the 'and so ons'.

Zen became an ally but didn't swallow me, it remained an experiment, a kind of art project which works with my waywardness. There is something magical about wandering free, even within the limitations that life brings and something about if your intentions are from the heart, you will find your way and find your luck.

Squash: The Walk was, as Madhead says and Roger alluded to, a means of escape. An escape from the hippie swamp, the lying in rooms stoned saying "I'm really stoned man" and doing not much else. I hated that, the idea that getting stoned was an end in itself. To me the point of getting stoned was to be out and about, experiencing a slightly altered reality. But for me the Walk was not just an escape *from*, it was more importantly an escape *to* the rest of my life, leaving my young self and taking the first steps to being a fully functioning man and finding out what that would mean. A different kind of man from the men that went before. There was a lot of unravelling for me to do, unpicking the "glorious" story of Britain and Empire, relations between men and women, realising that our much-vaunted freedoms were still just so much slavery, wage-slavery if you like – and so many things that needed to be changed in us and in the world.

As Pink Floyd sang *"the memories of a man in his old age are the deeds of a man in his prime"*.∗ Let that be a lesson to young people everywhere to lay up deeds while you can.

* "Free Four" from the 1972 album *Obscured by Clouds* by Pink Floyd

I sit here now, an old man, looking back and thinking yes this was a good thing to do and was made a wonderful thing to do with such special friends and companions. The following 50 years of my life were dedicated, in my own way, to trying to become a better person and make the world a better place and were built on the strong and trustworthy foundations laid down so solidly by The Long Walk to Glastonbury.

The Long Walk to Glastonbury campsites

For anyone who yearns to replicate the Long Walk (unlikely I know) here is the whole route we took showing where we laid our heads each night. Like you, I wonder if it is even possible now without getting shot at, arrested or driven away.

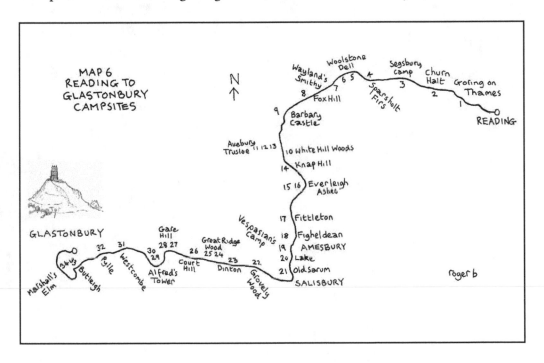

The Long Walk to Glastonbury menu

Many of the responses to the Long Walk to Glastonbury when it was serialised on Facebook concerned questions about our diet. Many people wondered particularly where we were able to obtain in 1973 such exotic ingredients as miso paste, hiziki and wakame seaweed and ginseng. The answer is that Roger got them from a secret place that neither Madhead or I knew. He carried them in a magic pouch that kept on producing.

Further thanks are due to Roger for compiling the following list of everything we ate on the Walk. He was fascinated by how the Diary recorded the details of our sustenance. These were all lifted from the text, roughly in order of breakfast lunch and dinner or not. If anyone wants to repeat the adventure, here is what you get to eat. Perhaps someone could conduct a science experiment into the nutritional value of this diet to see if it is possible for humans to survive for 35 days on this food. *

beer not included

Day	Menu
1	Stinging nettle tops to add to the bubbling brown rice
2	Muesli and stewed tea
	Wakame seaweed, leather top mushrooms, carrots, spuds and celery all stewed up with miso served with a hunk of bread
3	Muesli and hot milk
	Bread, cheese and pickled onions
4	Roasted sesame seeds, brown rice, carrots, onions, and nettle tops
5	Muesli, campfire-toasted bread and miso
	Miso stew with vegetables and seaweed, ginseng

6	Scrambled eggs
	Mashed swede and potatoes, sesame seeds, miso, seaweed and bread
7	Tea and biscuits.
	Wrinkled swedes boiled up with carrots and onions with Marmite and miso, steamed nettle tops and a hunk of cheese and bread
	Ice cream cornet
	Tea and crunchy peanut butter sandwiches
8	Roasted sesame seeds, brown rice, potatoes, onions, cheese and miso
9	Salty porridge with raisins and Mu tea
	Swizzels lollies. Ginger cake
	Boiled onions, carrots and peas, marmite, bread and cheese
10	Oats, nuts and raisins with hot milk
	Egg chips and beans, fried bread, bread and butter, rhubarb pie and custard, a bun and five cups of tea
	Ploughman's lunch
11	Egg chips and beans
12	Sworn-at porridge with unabused raisins
	Cheese, bread, pickled onions, mushrooms and a banana
13	Weetabix with thick gold top milk
	Tea and cakes.
	Boiled rice, onions and potatoes, lentils, hiziki seaweed, brown bread and miso
14	Weetabix with nuts and raisins
	Cheese and biscuits
	Vicarage tea and scones
	Egg fried rice and miso vegetable stew
15	Boiled eggs and bread, amazing thick sweet porridge with raisins
16	Japanese breakfast of onions, potatoes, lentils, green peppers, buckwheat, masses of miso, lashings of tea
	Bisk-o-Weet
	Cheese and bread and peanut butter and Marmite and apple
17	Bisk-O-Weet, raisins and walnuts
	Potato, carrot, hiziki, onion stew, buckwheat, apple, bread and Marmite
18	Porridge, buckwheat and raisins
	Rice and lentils, sardines, onion, bread

19	Rice and lentils with potatoes and onions, bashed up with miso paste, bread and cheese
20	Rice and lentils, potatoes and onions, cheese and bread
21	Porridge and buckwheat and a bowl of tea Rice, lentils, vegetables, hiziki, miso, cheese
22	Cold oats, buckwheat and raisins Bread, Yeastrel and peanut butter Burnt rice, lentils, potatoes and onions, Yeastrel A third of an orange each
23	Cold feast of oats, buckwheat, nuts and raisins Wholemeal bread and margarine and Yeastrel and peanut butter Rice and lentils, onions, carrots, hiziki and miso followed by stewed rhubarb with some sugar
24	Muesli Half a small Hovis each with peanut butter and Yeastrel followed by half an orange. Rice and lentils, carrots and potatoes, miso
25	Muesli Shared a pint of gold top milk and a Bounty bar Rice, potatoes, cheese and the inside of our burnt Scofa loaf, followed by tea and chocolate
26	Muesli Hovis, fish paste, Yeastrel and half an orange each. An ice cream each. Shared a Milky Way our chocolate transport to the stars Rice, lentils, potatoes, carrots, miso and cheese
27	Muesli Shared a Mars Bar. Bread, lettuce, fish paste and Yeastrel, followed by half an orange each Rice, lentils, potatoes, cheese followed by sugar sandwiches
28	Muesli Brown bread, Yeastrel, fish paste and half an orange each. Mashed potatoes, lentils, carrots, hiziki, miso and bread
29	Muesli Bread, lettuce, Yeastrel, fish paste, half an orange and half a Mars Bar each. Rice, potatoes, carrots, miso

30	Muesli.
	Bread and Shippam's Bloater Paste with chip butties
	Ice lollies and a Mars Bar
	Toast and bloater paste
31	Muesli
	Lentils, spuds, carrots, miso, old manky cheese
32	Muesli
	Manky cheese sandwich with peppery nasturtium leaves. Chips to follow
	Rice and lentils, potato and carrot with miso and cheese
33	Muesli
	Shared apple
	Hovis Roundy bread with something probably
	Muesli and a sandwich each with cucumber
34	Muesli with sliced apple
	Ice creams
	Pickled eggs
	White rice, lentils, potatoes and carrots, spring onion stalks, miso and cheese
35	Muesli
	Malt loaf and dates and a drink of metallic water from the Chalice Well

Printed in the USA
CPSIA information can be obtained
at www.ICGtesting.com
LVHW081650100923
757787LV00036B/441

9 781803 523002